Practical Gardeners' Guides

THE GREENHOUSE GARDEN

Peter Blackburne-Maze
Ken March

CONTENTS

CHOOSING A GREENHOUSE	4
EQUIPPING THE GREENHOUSE	8
POTS AND COMPOSTS	16
PLANNING WHAT TO GROW	20
ROUTINE CARE	22
A-Z OF FOLIAGE PLANTS	30
A-Z OF FLOWERING PLANTS	44
A-Z OF FRUIT AND VEGETABLES	62
A-Z OF CLIMBING PLANTS	72
INDEX	78

NOTES
For convenience, ease of growing symbols have been incorporated in the A-Z sections.
They can be interpreted as follows:
　*Easy to grow plants
　**Plants which require more than average care
***Temperamental or difficult to grow plants
These symbols are appropriate as long as the correct conditions are
provided.

This edition published in 1989
by Octopus Books Limited,
a division of the Octopus Publishing Group,
Michelin House,
81 Fulham Road,
London SW3 6RB

Copyright © Cathay Books, 1983

ISBN 0 7064 2587 1

Produced by Mandarin Offset
Printed and bound in Hong Kong

CHOOSING A GREENHOUSE

A greenhouse can open up a whole new world of gardening to anyone interested in plants, and it is an investment that will provide years of pleasure. You do not have to spend a fortune heating it either – even an unheated greenhouse can provide lots of interest, and just keeping it frost-free will widen the possibilities enormously.

A heated greenhouse will enable you to grow a whole range of plants that you would not be able to cultivate in the open – not just the 'exotics' but also many 'houseplants' as well as some fruit and vegetables. It can also be used to protect plants throughout the winter that are too delicate to stay outside.

There is also the possibility of raising your own bedding plants, and you can give vegetables like sweet corn and runner beans an early start.

Once you decide to buy a greenhouse, it is important to consider where to site it. Obviously much depends on the size and shape of your garden, but the following considerations should be taken into account:

- The position must receive the maximum amount of light. If possible it should run from north to south so that each side catches the sun, although with the narrow glazing bars of most modern greenhouses this is not too important, and opinions differ as to the best aspect.
- Make sure the site is not shaded by overhanging branches of trees or tall fences.
- Avoid a windy site. Shelter is essential as wind has a serious cooling effect.
- If you want to have mains water or electricity laid on, you should choose a place close to a source. It will reduce the cost of installation.
- A greenhouse should never dominate a garden, nor interfere with its ease of upkeep. Make sure it does not create awkward little corners that are difficult to look after.
- To reduce breakages, avoid a site anywhere near an area where children are likely to play ball games.
- The site should be level so that the greenhouse is easy to erect. This also ensures that water and cold air do not collect at one end.

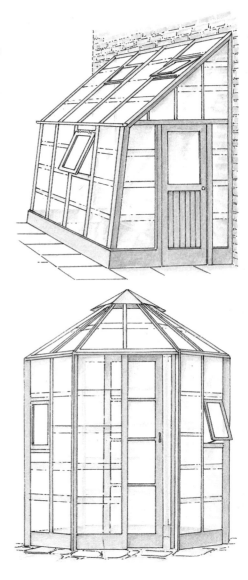

Lean-to (top) and circular (bottom) greenhouses are very useful in small gardens. The lean-to uses less material than a standard type and is frequently warmer; a circular greenhouse is convenient to work in and it can hold more plants than a conventional greenhouse.

FREE-STANDING OR LEAN-TO?

Although a free-standing greenhouse is likely to give you more growing space, you might like to consider a lean-to. These have many advantages: they are usually close to a water and electricity supply; heat 'stored' in the house wall reduces heating costs; the greenhouse has the convenience of being close at hand (you can even have a door directly into it from the house). Their main disadvantage is the limited choice that you have in positioning them, and the possibility that they will not face in the best direction for catching the sun.

In any case, there will not be as much light for the plants as in a free-standing model.

SIZE AND SHAPE

Deciding how large the greenhouse should be is never easy, but you should try to buy the largest you can afford, bearing in mind the other factors and the cost of heating. Most gardeners grow far more plants than their greenhouse will comfortably hold, so the larger it is the less likely you are to be frustrated.

Shape is usually of less importance. In theory, the nearer a greenhouse is to circular, the better the light admission, but making your own fixtures and fittings for it is very tricky unless you are a master-carpenter or a metal-worker. Rectangular greenhouses with straight sides make best use of benching and shelving, while those with sloping sides are claimed to admit more light.

WOOD OR METAL?

Probably the most vexed question of all is the initial choice between a wooden greenhouse and a metal one.

Wood is a soft material into which screws, nails, hooks, and so on, can easily be driven. This makes it simple to fix training wires, polythene linings and anything else that you might want to (although you can buy attachments that make all these things possible in most metal greenhouses). Wood is also a 'warmer' material than metal, and wooden greenhouses may retain a little more heat than metal-framed ones.

Whether stained or painted, a wooden greenhouse normally looks more in keeping with a garden. This may, at first, seem a small point but since everything in a garden should contribute to its attractiveness, it is important to consider the appearance of the greenhouse. The greater weight of a wooden structure adds to its stability in storms and gales.

There are, however, disadvantages to wooden greenhouses. They require much more maintenance than their metal counterparts to prevent deterioration. Wooden greenhouses are also flammable – a point not to be overlooked, especially if you intend to use a paraffin heater.

Metal-framed greenhouses have narrower glazing bars, and this admits more light. Very little maintenance is required in comparison with wood, and metal has a longer life, even if not looked after.

As regards the types of metal used for making greenhouses, aluminum alloy is an infinitely better material than steel. Steel is extremely heavy and its hardness makes the installation of any extras a major operation.

HOW EASY TO ERECT?

It is, of course, also necessary to consider the ease with which the greenhouse can be put up. The types and sizes that most gardeners buy come in various stages of pre-construction; some metal ones look like giant Meccano sets, whereas wooden ones are often delivered by the manufacturer with the two roof sections, the sides, and the ends already assembled. These wooden ones are fairly easy to put up, but the glazing, which has to be done with putty, takes a lot longer than it does with metal greenhouses. In these the individual sheets of glass are usually held in place by clips. From start to finish, however, the two sorts probably take about the same time to erect.

GLAZING MATERIALS

Except where breakages are likely to be frequent, glass is still the best value for money. Even in an unheated greenhouse, it can keep out something like 5°C (10°F) of frost. It has excellent light admission and, within limits, its strength is good. It is also relatively cheap. There are several rigid or semi-rigid plastics on the market but, for one reason or another (usually cost), they fail to match up to glass except in strength. Polythene is becoming a popular glazing material and is certainly cheaper than glass, but heat is not retained so well

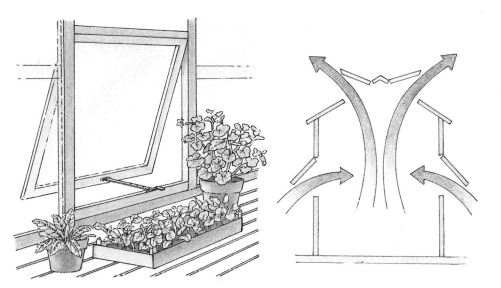

Good ventilation is essential in a greenhouse if the plants are to flourish. Not only does it help to keep them cool in the summer, it also encourages good air circulation, a vital part of pest and disease control. For maximum efficiency, ventilators should be fully adjustable and open as widely as possible. To ensure thorough air circulation, ventilators should be fitted in the sides of the greenhouse, as well as the roof.

and it has to be replaced every one to three years. If you do use polythene, make sure it is a heavy (thick) gauge and treated with an ultraviolet light inhibitor (often called UVI polythene).

Under normal conditions, glass is the best material. For greenhouse purposes it is usually 3 mm thick (⅛ inch). Do make sure that the system for replacing broken panes is straightforward, for breakages inevitably occur.

VENTILATORS
Ventilation is essential to the efficient working of the greenhouse, yet it is rarely given sufficient thought at the planning stage. All too many greenhouses are simply equipped with a ridge ventilator on each side of the roof. This is fine from the point of view of letting hot air escape and for preventing the temperature from rising too high, but it does little to keep the plants themselves cool; the only fresh air in the greenhouse is that which flows from one ventilator to the other.

The best way of overcoming this so that there is fresh air amongst the plants is to make sure that the greenhouse has side ventilators at about bench height. This will also give you far greater control over the temperature inside the greenhouse. At the same time it is important to avoid draughts, as these can be detrimental to many plants.

It is well worth considering louvre vents for the side of the greenhouse.

GUTTERS
Gutters are not essential, particularly if you are trying to keep the price down, but they are useful. Convenient though they may be for collecting rainwater, the amount you can save off a small greenhouse roof is never likely to be enough for watering the plants throughout the summer so its main job is to prevent drips outside the house. Judge for yourself how necessary this is.

SHOPPING AROUND
The key points to consider have been outlined in this chapter, but it must be emphasized that the only sensible way to decide is to inspect and compare as many models as you can. Only then can you select one that suits your requirements.

EQUIPPING THE GREENHOUSE

Once you become the proud owner of a green-house the obvious question arises as to how much and what equipment you should install. This chapter steers you through the many greenhouse accessories so that you can decide which are important to you and which are nice to have but by no means essential if you cannot afford them yet.

BENCHES AND SHELVING

Sometimes benching is included in the price of the greenhouse, but often it is an optional extra. This, of course, should be taken into account when comparing prices.

A greenhouse should have benching on one side at least. The other side can be used for tomatoes, cucumbers, and other large plants. On the other hand if you want to concentrate on pot plants you will probably need benches on both sides.

The decision is not one that need be made when buying the greenhouse – there are sever-al types of benching or 'staging' that can be bought 'off the peg', later. These can be adapted to the size of your greenhouse and can be put up and taken down as required. It is also perfectly possible and quite easy, with a few tools, to make your own.

The choice of materials is between wood and metal again, and the pros and cons are similar to those already mentioned for the greenhouse itself. If you are making your own, however, wood is much easier to work.

You may consider having a corrugated asbestos top to the benching. This is fine pro-vided you get the kind with narrow corruga-tions; if it has wide ones, you will run into trouble with small pots tipping over, although this can always be prevented by spreading fine shingle over the asbestos. Something else worth doing is drilling holes in the 'troughs' to allow surplus water to drain away. *Caution:* wear protective clothing and a face mask when drilling into asbestos as the dust may be harm-ful, especially if inhaled.

In the spring, you may want to erect temporary shelving to house all the pots and boxes of seedlings. These will greatly increase the capacity of the greenhouse at a time when space is at a premium.

If planks are used for the shelves, they should be about 18 cm (7 inches) wide and 2 cm (¾ inch) thick. These shelves will comfortably hold two 9 cm (3½ inch) pots across as well as seed trays and will be amply strong provided they are supported by metal brackets every 60 cm (2 ft) or so, though the exact measure-ment will depend on the distance between the glazing bars.

You can, of course, buy aluminium shelves that are easily fixed to most aluminium alloy greenhouses with the special nuts and bolts provided.

If the top shelf is positioned about 7 cm (3 inches) below the eaves, it can be left in place and used as an anchor point for strings to support tomatoes and cucumbers when the staging underneath has been removed. Alternatively, a strong wire can be run from one end of the greenhouse to the other, with several fixing points in between, and the sup-port strings tied to this.

Careful planning and tidiness are essential if your greenhouse is to be used efficiently. A clean, tidy interior also discourages pests and diseases.

FLOORS

This may sound rather an elementary subject but a greenhouse should always have a proper 'floor' – rather than packed mud with a profusion of weeds growing in it! The ideal material is properly laid concrete, as it is firm to walk on, can easily be scrubbed when it threatens to become slippery with green algae, and it is weed free. Paving slabs are also good, provided they are laid evenly on a bed of sand.

At a pinch, duck-boards can be used but they have the serious disadvantage that they can harbour pests and diseases, whilst the soil beneath them is often thick with weeds. Also, their life is apt to be short unless they are treated with a preservative at least once a year. This must not be creosote, whose fumes would damage or even kill the plants, but a copper-based preservative safe for use near plants.

The extent of the flooring need not be great; a walkway down the centre of the greenhouse between the two sets of staging is enough. Under the staging, the ground should be kept weed-free either by spreading shingle over it or by an occasional hoeing. Where appropriate, you could even grow tender ground cover plants in it; they would need very little attention as all their water and food would probably come as drainage water from above (but not if you use a capillary watering system).

It is a good idea to have a path leading into the greenhouse as well as a floor inside, as this will stop mud from being walked in.

INSULATION

With the ever-increasing cost of heating, anything that can be done to cut down the heat loss in winter is likely to pay for itself in the first season or two. As in the home, some form of double glazing is the answer, coupled with the careful control of heating.

You can buy a fully double-glazed greenhouse that uses glass. Both full-span and lean-to models are available, and the larger ones can have two compartments, either or both of which can be double glazed. Although excellent value for money, these are towards the top end of the market and most gardeners will be looking for something that they can do relatively cheaply themselves. Plastic insulating materials can easily be fixed to wooden greenhouses, and to aluminium alloy greenhouses

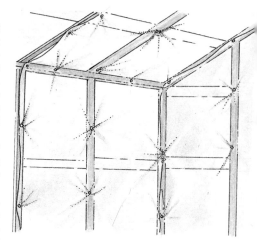

with special fixings that are readily available.

The cheapest form of double glazing is polythene sheeting fixed to the inside of the greenhouse (with drawing pins in a timber-framed greenhouse). The ventilators must be done separately otherwise you will not be able to open them.

Any kind of polythene lining will encourage condensation, but careful use of the ventilators and sensible watering should keep it to a minimum. The trouble with condensation is that it frequently drips onto the plants at a time when the foliage should be kept dry to reduce the risk of fungus diseases.

A more recent material that has much better insulating properties and is not so prone to condensation is 'bubble plastic'. This was originally designed as a packaging material instead of wood shavings but has since been developed as an insulator with larger bubbles. Although double skinned, the light admission is still good.

There is no specific time during which a polythene lining should be in place but it is usual to insulate the greenhouse from October or November to March or April.

VENTILATION

Ventilators are designed to control the heat within a greenhouse, so clearly they should be opened when a certain temperature is reached and closed again when it drops below that temperature. To do this manually would be a full-time job.

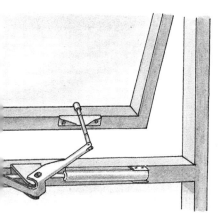

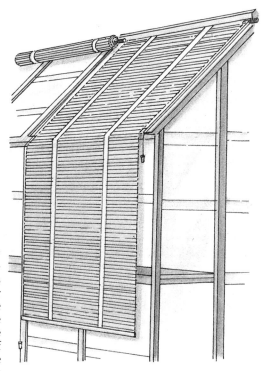

To overcome this problem, there are now automatic ventilator openers. These are completely self-contained, and no electricity is needed to work them: a fluid in a cylinder expands and contracts with changes in the temperature to move the operating arm. The whole system can be adjusted to open and close at any reasonable temperature. The more of these automatic openers that you fit to the greenhouse, the greater your control over the temperature, but most gardeners achieve reasonable control with just one.

An automatic ventilator will stop the temperature rising too high early on a summer's morning before you are up and about, and it will also close the greenhouse down in the late evening.

Of all the equipment that can be bought for a greenhouse, this is probably the most worthwhile as it saves a lot of work and worry, and is certainly beneficial for the plants.

SHADING

Along with the correct use of ventilators, shading is another means of controlling the temperature in a greenhouse.

The simplest and cheapest form comes in a tin or bottle and you paint it on like whitewash. The major drawback to this is that, once put on in the spring, it is there come rain or shine until you wash or rub it off in the autumn. It will certainly cut down the amount of sunlight that enters the greenhouse on a bright day, and this will keep the temperature down and prevent scorch. This disadvantage is that it also restricts

Although polythene lining (left) conserves a great deal of heat in the winter, keeping the plants cool in summer is just as important. Automatic ventilators (middle) and roller blinds (right) make this simple.

the light admission on dull days.

Whilst this 'liquid shading' is perfectly adequate for many gardeners, something rather more versatile and sophisticated is obviously better. Many types of blind can be bought, from the wooden slat kind to a simple small-mesh netting. Provided that the blinds cut out about a third of the direct sunlight, the real choice rests on how much you are prepared to pay and how easy to work you want the system to be.

The slatted kind is usually fitted with cords and pulleys to make raising and lowering it easy, whereas the netting comes in rolls from which you cut out panels of the correct size. With a bit of ingenuity, you can easily devise a way of operating this type, with wooden battens at the top and bottom of the netting.

HEATING

Even if you start off without any form of heating, the time will soon come when its advantages become apparent. If you want to get the most out of your greenhouse, however, there is much to be said for heating it right from the start. The actual choice of system depends on many things, such as the amount of heat required, the type of fuel and the cost of the heater – including how much it might cost to install and how much it will cost to run.

In the past, a coal- or coke-burning boiler feeding 10 cm (4 inch) hot-water pipes was the standard way of heating a greenhouse. Today, the vast majority of heaters warm the air directly rather than indirectly. These systems are far cheaper to install and their effect is more instant as there is little 'warming up' period.

The basic choice is between electricity, propane gas and paraffin.

Electrical heaters are the most expensive to buy, but they are clean to handle, are completely free of fumes, and are almost always fitted with a thermostat – which gives a more even temperature and avoids wasting fuel. Tubular heaters are very effective, and give a surprisingly even distribution of heat. You may, however, prefer a fan heater as these respond quickly and can be used to keep cold air moving in summer. For both types you will, of course, need an electricity supply in the greenhouse. A disadvantage of electric heaters is their vulnerability to power cuts, and unfortunately these are most likely to occur during the crucial winter months. There are many models and types of electrical heaters, so it pays to look at several before you decide on which one to buy.

Propane gas heaters can be run quite cheaply, and will provide a wide range of heat with little risk of harmful fumes, although water vapour is produced as with paraffin, and again some ventilation is generally advisable. The drawback of butane heaters is that they are cumbersome, and unless a pressure gauge is fitted they can run out of gas before you realize it. Also the replacement cylinders are heavy to carry. Many butane heaters include a thermostat.

Paraffin heaters are the cheapest to buy and can cost relatively little to run if you are just trying to keep the greenhouse frost-free. Against this is the fairly frequent filling they need, the messiness of paraffin, and the risk of damaging

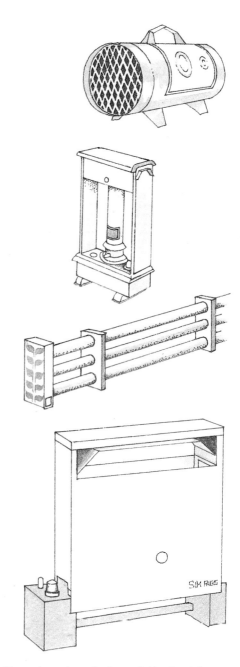

Types of greenhouse heater available: electric fan heater, paraffin heater, tubular electric heater, propane gas heater.

fumes if the wick is badly set. It is possible to buy a paraffin heater with a thermostat, but these models are not widely available.

Paraffin heaters produce water vapour that leads to increased condensation, and wherever combustible fuels are used, some ventilation should be provided to enable fresh air to enter the greenhouse. For safety's sake these heaters must be used carefully.

In summary: Electrical heaters are the most convenient but the most expensive to run. Paraffin heaters are cheap to buy and are usually adequate for a small greenhouse. Propane heaters are efficient but are apt to be bulky.

Size of heater: Having decided on the type of heater you prefer, the important thing is that you buy one powerful enough to heat your greenhouse to the sort of temperature you need. If you settle for one that will have to work flat out the whole time to maintain the temperature, there will be nothing in reserve if the outside temperature drops to the kind of level that it did in the winter of 1981-82. On the other hand, a heater that is capable of producing far more heat than is required will not only be more expensive to buy than a smaller and more appropriate one but it will generally be harder to keep the temperature down to a reasonable level. It is important to try to maintain an even winter temperature, especially if plants are in a dormant state.

PROPAGATORS

These are extremely handy if you want to raise a lot of plants from cuttings; and they are also useful for germinating seeds at any time of the year when the temperature within the greenhouse is too low.

Most propagators consist of a container very similar to a seed tray that is fitted with a transparent plastic lid. The tray is normally filled with a peat and sand mixture in which the cuttings are rooted, and the lid is put in place to maintain the temperature and a humid atmosphere.

Although many cuttings can be rooted without a propagator, it will greatly increase the chances of success and the range of 'rootable' plants. In addition, it will avoid the need to heat the whole greenhouse to the temperature required for rooting or germination, which means a considerable saving in fuel.

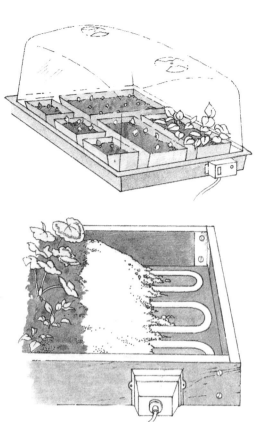

Readymade propagators with electrical soil warming cables are available (top). Alternatively you can make your own (bottom).

Propagators are available in many sizes and are made of several kinds of plastic as well as aluminium. However, they are usually one of two types: electrical ones that contain a heating element, and plain, unheated ones. You can, however, buy one that sits over a paraffin heater. Obviously heated propagators have a big advantage over the others and, if you can afford one and put it to good use, it is well worth the cost: it provides you with a mini greenhouse within the main one.

Most propagators are fitted with adjustable vents in the lid. Although these are certainly an advantage they are not essential. It is important to choose a fairly robust model because the cheaper ones tend to break all too easily.

You can, of course, make your own propagator, or even a heated bench. These can be heated with soil-warming cables buried in the peat and sand in the bottom. They are not difficult to use, and are fairly cheap to run.

WATERING DEVICES

The final 'extra' you might like to consider is automatic or semi-automatic watering.

A number of systems are available that work on the 'drip' principle in which a separate tube is led into each pot or tray from a larger pipe connected to a tap or reservoir in the greenhouse. This is a very efficient method if you have a lot of plants that all need the same amount of water at the same time. If you are growing a mixed collection, which is far more likely, it needs a certain amount of adapting otherwise some plants get flooded whilst others are still too dry.

A more practical system involves the use of capillary matting. This is a sort of blanket, which you keep saturated with water and on which the pots and trays are stood so that each one can soak up as much water as it needs. Not only does this eliminate hand watering but it also encourages far better plants, as they have as much water as they need without ever becoming waterlogged. Liquid feeding is best done by hand every so often but this is a small penalty to pay for the convenience. You can introduce the feed into the water supply, but there are drawbacks to this. The snag with capillary watering is that the plants might be too wet in winter.

When setting up a capillary system, the first essential is to have a waterproof base on which to lay the matting. This can be watered by hand when required, or you can set up a system of wicks leading to it from a basin of water. However, the basin should never be higher than the matting or a syphoning action will be set up which empties the basin and floods the matting. Or it can be fed from a special reservoir that you can buy.

Another way is to fill a gallon cider jar, invert it quickly and put the open end on a corner of the matting. As the matting dries, air gets into the jar and water glugs out until the matting is saturated again. Provided these systems are set up carefully, they can be very efficient, but as hand watering the matting takes so little time

their main benefit is only apparent if you have to leave the greenhouse unattended.

The forerunner of capillary matting, the sand bench, can also be made fully automatic. Fine sand is laid down in the same way as the matting and a level pipe is led into it from a cistern attached to the end of the bench. The cistern is linked to the mains through a ball-cock (or you can use a hand-filled reservoir) and as the level of water in the sand drops, more flows in. The art here is to place the cistern and adjust the valve so that the water level in the sand is exactly the same as that in the tank.

With any form of capillary watering, the three essentials are a completely level bench, a watertight base, and good contact between the matting or sand and the compost in the pot (which means that no crocks should be put in the bottom of pots).

MAINS WATER AND ELECTRICITY

Soil-warming cables, fan heaters, and propagators need a power supply, and some automatic watering systems need a mains water connection. Installing an electricity and water supply can be expensive, but they are not jobs to be economized on by doing them yourself. If there are any faults with wiring or fittings, the results could be fatal. Always enlist the help of a professional. *You have been warned!*

OTHER EQUIPMENT

Although various other gadgets, such as mist propagators, are available, those dealt with here are the ones that are most likely to be of use when you first buy a greenhouse; the others will come later as you build up experience and want to branch out. Above all, stay clear of equipment that is unlikely to justify its expense. Only buy those things that are going to be genuinely useful.

Although a wide variety of gadgets is available, it is perfectly possible to equip a greenhouse with simple, inexpensive items. Whether you use a fully automatic or a semi-automatic watering system, or simply a can, always aim to provide the plants with as much water as they need, but no more.

POTS AND COMPOSTS

Besides all the other little things that you will be using in the greenhouse, such as a dibber, watering-can, a presser board for firming the compost in pots and seed trays, a sprayer, plant labels, and split-canes for supporting tall plants, the most important items are likely to be pots and seed trays. As there are many types it pays to know what to look for when you buy them.

Pots were traditionally made from clay and seed trays from wood, but these have both been challenged by plastics. Which is best depends partly on what you want to grow and partly on personal preferences. Trial and error will probably determine which is the best for you, but the following pros and cons should alert you to the strengths and weaknesses of each.

CLAY POTS

Being porous, clay pots make it less likely that you will overwater the plants, and because of thickness, they also have a greater buffering effect against changes in temperature. They are also relatively heavy so that tall plants are less likely to topple over. They are often preferred simply for their appearance, which is usually more pleasing than plastic.

Against this has to be considered their greater weight when handling them in quantity and the fact that they take up much more room in storage. Some people regard them as more easily broken and, whilst this is undoubtedly true if you drop them, in other respects they are just as strong as plastic, and often stronger. A possible disadvantage of their porosity is that the compost in them will dry out quicker, but this depends on the method of watering you adopt; in the winter, drying out is certainly no problem. They are more difficult to scrub clean than plastic.

PLASTIC POTS

The thing to remember about plastic pots is that they vary enormously in quality, depending on the type of plastic from which they are made. The best sort is almost certainly polypropylene as it combines strength with semi-rigidity. So often you find pots that are either floppy or

brittle; both are equally useless and are priced accordingly. Plastic pots are easy to handle in bulk and well-designed ones take up very little room when stacked. Good plastic pots are almost indestructible and are unaffected by extremes of temperature. They are frequently available in colours other than terra-cotta.

The main disadvantages of plastic pots are that tall plants are often top-heavy in them, and that you have to water the plants more carefully in the winter as the compost does not dry out so readily.

PEAT POTS AND BLOCKS

For seedlings that are to be planted outdoors or in the greenhouse border later, you can use peat pots or blocks. Most peat pots – and pots made from other materials that will allow the roots to grow through – are difficult to keep moist in the small sizes, but have the merit of causing

Peat blocks are most useful for growing seedlings, such as tomatoes and bedding plants, that are to be planted into the greenhouse border or into larger pots or growing bags later. A peat block compressor or 'blocking tool' is used to press out blocks from a special peat compost.

little root disturbance when the seedlings are eventually planted out. An alternative to peat pots are peat blocks, which you press out from a special peat compost using a 'blocking' tool. These blocks take up little room on the bench, and make transplanting easy. However, you really need to use a capillary watering system otherwise the blocks are likely to dry out and check the growth of the seedlings.

You can use small expandable peat 'pellets' to sow pot-plant seedlings into. These can then be potted up into an ordinary pot without the root disturbance caused by pricking out.

SEED TRAYS

To say that there is a choice of materials is somewhat misleading, as wooden ones have all but disappeared. They are certainly not as long-lasting as good plastic trays, and they take up a lot more storage room. But they do have the big advantage that they are rigid. This may not seem important but it does mean that they can be moved about with plants in them without twisting. The factors concerning the different types of plastic are the same as for pots.

COMPOSTS

The compost that interests the greenhouse gardener has nothing to do with the garden compost heap. Potting compost should always be made carefully from special ingredients.

Composts can be divided into three types: seed or sowing compost, potting compost, and all-purpose compost. The first is for raising young plants from seeds or cuttings; potting compost is for growing on plants of any age that already have an established root system; all-purpose compost can be used for raising plants and for growing them on.

The reason for having different composts for sowing and growing is that plant foods are required in varying amounts by seedlings (or rooted cuttings) and older plants. All-purpose composts are something of a compromise, but are perfectly suitable for the vast majority of gardeners; all-purpose composts are likely to be peat-based.

Soil-less composts can be made from peat alone, but usually include sand, vermiculite or perlite. Loam-based composts, such as the John Innes range, depend on soil as the key constituent. Soil-less composts are certainly lighter to carry and handle, and because all the ingredients are naturally sterile there is little risk of plant diseases being carried by them. The majority are mass-produced. This, and the fact that there is very little variation in the raw materials, more or less guarantees that, for a given brand, the compost is going to be the same wherever and whenever you buy it. Against this are the drawbacks: peat-based composts are more difficult to 'manage' (they are more easily over- or underwatered) and they soon run out of nutrients, so you will probably have to feed your plants sooner than you would with a loam-based compost.

If you want to use a loam-based compost, one made to the John Innes formula (it is not a brand) is almost certainly your best choice – although quality can vary. John Innes composts are less susceptible to under-feeding as there is always a certain reservoir of nutrients in the

loam. They are also better for permanent large plants as their extra weight and density add stability and reduce the likelihood of top-heaviness.

The shortage of suitable loam can tempt some manufacturers to take short cuts, which result in an inferior compost. This has to some extent been overcome by the setting up of the John Innes Manufacturers' Association – their bags carry a seal of approval. Members of the association are bound by a code of conduct to stick to the original specifications – though even this is no absolute guarantee of quality. There have been improvements in fertilizer technology, however, and slow-release fertilizers are sometimes used (normally the compost can deteriorate after a few weeks because of chemical reactions). Alternatively it is possible to buy a compost to which you add the fertilizer provided before use.

There are four basic 'grades' of John Innes compost: one for seeds (seed compost) and three for potting (potting composts 1, 2, 3). No. 2 contains twice as much fertilizer as No. 1 and No. 3 contains three times as much. There are special mixes for lime-hating plants.

HOME-MADE COMPOSTS

Although ready-made composts are by no means cheap, it is folly to run the risk of failure by making your own special 'brew'; you will very likely be throwing away the cost of the seeds as well. Provided you buy a reliable brand of compost, you have the assurance that you are getting something of high quality that will do the job it is intended for.

It is, however, possible to buy a proprietary DIY compost kit that provides the necessary ingredients. This might be worth trying as there is no guesswork on your part – the right amount of fertilizer will be provided – but follow any instructions carefully.

It is most unwise to try to make your own compost using unsterilized loam, because pests and diseases can easily be introduced by doing so.

LOAM-BASED OR SOIL-LESS?

Both types of compost have their advantages and disadvantages, but either is suitable for the vast majority of plants. On the whole, however, the soil-less ones probably have more advantages, though they do need more careful handling. Once they are mastered, the plants grown in them are frequently better.

Another development of soil-less composts has, over the last seven or eight years, been introduced to the gardening public in the shape of growing bags. These have several advantages over traditional ways of growing many greenhouse crops as well as being equally suitable for use outdoors.

One of the big problems with using the greenhouse border for crops year after year is that, to be safe from soil-borne pests and diseases, the soil has to be changed or sterilized at least every other year, and preferably annually. Growing bags avoid the need for this as the plants in them are completely isolated from whatever lies underneath. They are quite expensive, but very convenient, and you will probably end up producing much better crops.

PLANNING WHAT TO GROW

Important though equipment and aids are, greenhouse gardening is about growing plants – and few decisions can be as important as which plants to grow. The A-Z of greenhouse plants in this book will show you what you can reasonably expect to succeed with, but you also need to take into account space and timing as well as things like the temperature you can maintain.

Space can be at a premium at any time, but particularly so in spring when you will be raising a lot of plants that are to go outside later on when the risk of frosts is over. For this reason alone, early sowing is not always a good thing as the situation will arise when there are too many plants or they are too large for the greenhouse yet it will still not be safe to plant them outdoors.

Likewise, when any plants are at the correct stage for planting out in the greenhouse, it must be possible to do so. Here, though, we find one of the advantages of growing bags as these can be planted up and put in a temporary position in the greenhouse until the proper position becomes vacant.

Along with making sure that the greenhouse is never overcrowded comes the necessity of ensuring that it is always being used to the full.

When crops such as tomatoes, cucumbers, or melons are taking up one side, you will probably be using staging on the other to accommodate a succession of pot-plants for the home. These can start in the early spring with hardy annuals overwintered in pots, and carry right on through the primula species, calceolarias and cinerarias, ending up in the winter with cyclamen.

Never waste space. Chicory can easily be forced under the staging in winter.

GARDENING YEAR IN THE GREENHOU			
January	February	March	April
Keep cacti & succulents cool and dry			
Grow on bulbs until flowering finished			
		Sow calceolarias, celosia solanum, streptocarpus	
Keep foliage, flowering climbing plants on dry side			
Germinate outside vegetable plants from seed			
Germinate bedding plants from seed			
Keep apricots, grapes & peaches, cool and dry		Keep apri as require	
Sow aubergines, peppers & tomatoes			Pla
	Sow cucumbers		Pla
Sow melons			Pla
Grow and crop winter lettuces			
		Grow and crop spring & summe	
Force rhubarb			
Grow strawberries in growing bags until they h			

At some point in the year, time should also be set aside for moving out existing plants and cleaning the whole greenhouse thoroughly. The most convenient time for this is when the tomatoes, for example, have finished and very little is being propagated.

Winter is a time when greenhouses are more or less empty. Whilst this is quite normal, if you have to heat the greenhouse for some plants it is more economical to have as much growing as possible. Apart from the usual pot-plants, the space under the staging should be used for forcing crops like rhubarb and chicory. These are unlikely to interfere with anything else, even when the time comes for sowing in the spring.

Bulbs are always welcome and many of the smaller species of crocuses and narcissi can be grown in pots without any heat at all.

There are a great many different uses to which the greenhouse can be put. It is best to decide on the most important vegetable and decorative plants first, then fit the others in as time allows. The greenhouse planner (below) provides a valuable year-round guide to using your greenhouse.

May	June	July	August	September	October	November	December
...p cacti & succulents warmer, and water and feed →						Keep cacti & succulents cool and dry →	
					Plant spring bulbs →	Grow on bulbs →	
...d foliage, flowering & climbing plants and pot up ...necessary →						Keep foliage, flowering & climbing plants on dry side →	
...pagate foliage, flowering & climbing plants as ...uired →							
...es & peaches warmer; water more frequently and feed →						Keep apricots, grapes & peaches cool and dry →	
...feed aubergines, peppers & tomatoes as required →							
...feed cucumbers as required →							
...feed melons as required →							
					Grow and crop winter lettuces →		
...ttuce →							
...w mustard and cress as required at any time of the year →							
							Force rhubarb →
...ed fruiting →							

ROUTINE CARE

This chapter covers the routines that will help you to raise strong and healthy plants. As advice on individual plants will be found in the A-Z sections, this chapter deals mainly with principles.

PROPAGATION

Plants can be propagated in many ways – from seeds, from cuttings of various kinds, by division, or from plantlets for instance. Many plants are easy to propagate, but some need coaxing. If you follow the advice below you should not find much difficulty with most plants that you are likely to grow.

Before you try your hand at propagation, be warned: you will have some failures among your successes. Do not let this deter you.

New plants from seeds: This is by far the most common way of raising new plants, and in many cases it is Nature's way. There are three essentials for success:

- The seed must be viable (alive).
- It must be kept constantly damp, though not waterlogged or it will rot.
- It must have warmth, though the amount will vary with the species involved.

Once the seeds have germinated, they will also need light if they are to make good plants.

All you need for seed sowing is a suitable container and some seed compost. If there are a lot of seeds to sow, a seed tray will be needed, but a half-tray or even a pot will be sufficient if there are not many in the packet. When using a clay pot in conjunction with John Innes seed compost, place a piece of crock (broken pot) over the drainage hole to stop the compost running out, but it is not normally necessary with seed trays or plastic pots, nor if you use a soil-less compost.

Half fill with compost, lightly firm it and then carry on filling until the container is overfull. Strike the surface off level with the rim and press the compost down gently with a presser board.

When sowing very small seeds, like begonias, the best plan is to water the compost before you actually sow, but with larger seeds it need not be done until afterwards.

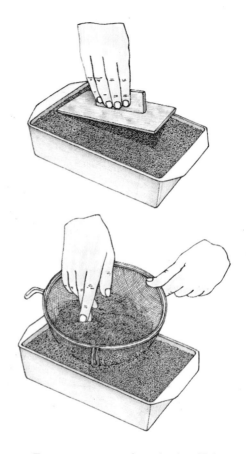

TOP: *To encourage even seed germination, fill the container with suitable compost and firm it lightly to give a level surface.*

BOTTOM: *After sowing the seeds thinly and evenly, sieve some more compost over them so that they are just buried.*

Sow the seeds thinly and evenly over the whole surface of the compost. Using a sieve, cover the seeds with compost until they are buried to about their own depth; very small seeds should not be covered at all. The pot or seed tray should be thoroughly wetted either by standing it in a dish of water until it shows moist at the surface, or by using a fine-rosed watering-can. Put some glass or polythene over the container and a sheet of newspaper on top of that, to keep the moisture in and reduce the chance of overheating. Place the pot or tray somewhere warm for the seeds to germinate.

Check it daily, and the moment you see signs of growth take off the newspaper; the glass or polythene can stay on until the seedlings are almost touching it. The seedlings must then be given full light to prevent straggly growth.

Cuttings: The parts of a plant normally used to provide cuttings include the top of the growing shoot (a stem cutting), sections of a shoot that include at least one leaf (a leaf-bud cutting), and with some plants the leaf itself (a leaf cutting). The conditions needed for a cutting to produce roots are similar to those required for seeds to germinate (warmth and moisture) but they also need plenty of light.

Stem cuttings should be 2.5-7.5 cm (1-3 inches) long, according to the species of plant, and are better if taken from non-flowering shoots. In the vast majority of cases the base of the cutting should be trimmed off neatly immediately below a leaf or pair of leaves (which are then removed). The bottom of the cutting may be dipped in hormone rooting powder or liquid to hasten rooting and then inserted into the compost as described later. Most of the common plants can be propagated in this way.

Leaf-bud cuttings are used primarily for climbers like ivy and are prepared by cutting a growing shoot into sections so that each section contains a leaf with a bud at its base. It is from this bud that the new plant will develop. So that there is a 'handle' for inserting the cutting and a 'peg' for holding it firmly in the compost, leave about 1 cm (½ inch) of stem above and below the leaf. The bottom half can then be dipped in hormone rooting powder and the cutting inserted so that the leaf-bud is just covered.

Leaf cuttings of plants like the African violet can, in fact, be rooted in water but they are often tricky to establish when finally put in potting

TOP: *Propagation by tip cuttings. A stem cutting with several leaves attached is taken from the top of a mature plant.*

CENTRE: *Cuttings are inserted into half-pots.*

BOTTOM: *Begonia rex can be propagated from leaf cuttings. A whole leaf is used.*

ABOVE: Chlorophytum (the spider plant) is particularly easy to propagate. Simply peg down the plantlets into their own pot of compost.

ABOVE: When growing plants from seed, they should be pricked out into fresh compost as soon as they are large enough to handle.

compost, so rooting them conventionally is usually better in the long run. With African violets, a whole mature leaf and leaf stalk is cut from the plant and inserted at an angle so that there is a small space between the blade and the compost.

A different technique is used for *Begonia rex*; a mature leaf is laid on the compost and pinned down. Each main vein is cut through and after a while, each of these areas will root and produce a new plant. Streptocarpus leaf cuttings are taken by cutting the leaf into sections, each about 2.5 cm (1 inch) wide. The bottom of each section is then gently pushed into the compost and the new plant develops from the buried portion of mid-rib.

When rooting cuttings, it helps to have a propagator for keeping them warm and moist, but you can use something like a gallon ice-cream tub with a transparent lid, putting a small amount of compost in the bottom, inserting the cuttings, and then putting on the lid. Alternatively, use an ordinary flower-pot and put the whole thing in a polythene bag after inserting the cuttings.

The compost you use is a matter of personal preference. You can root the cuttings in a seed compost, or you could try a mixture of 1 part peat and 1 part sharp sand.

When choosing part of a plant for cuttings, do make sure that it is healthy. Cuttings should be gently firmed in and then given a good watering before you enclose them.

The time taken to root will vary enormously, but is usually between two and four weeks for most plants. When they have rooted new growth will start to appear; this is the time when care is needed, as the rooted cuttings will have to be weaned gently to the less protected atmosphere of the rest of the greenhouse. This is done by gradually exposing them to more and more fresh air over a period of three or four days. At the end of this time, they should be ready for potting up.

Division: This method of propagation is used solely for plants that grow in clumps (like African violets). The plant is removed from its pot in the spring or early summer and gently teased apart into a number of smaller clumps. Each of these can be potted up. Many of the ferns are dealt with in this way, and it is a good way to propagate the yellow and green striped form of mother-in-law's tongue, as the yellow edge is lost if you take leaf cuttings.

Plantlets: Some houseplants increase their numbers naturally by producing mini-plants either on the end of flowering stems (notably the spider plant) or around the edges of the leaves (some bryophyllums). Once a plantlet is developing roots of its own, it can be parted from the parent, potted up in potting compost and kept in a close atmosphere for a few days until it is established.

Pricking out and potting up: As soon as seedlings are large enough to handle and cuttings have rooted, they must be removed into fresh

25

ABOVE: When first potting larger plants, pour the compost in evenly around the roots.

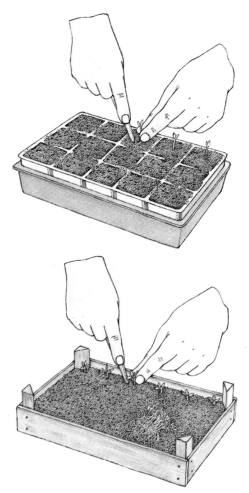

ABOVE: Peat pots are best for larger seedlings; smaller ones can be put straight into a tray.

compost. This can be of the all-purpose type or a specific soil-less or John Innes potting mixture. In the John Innes range, either No. 1 or No. 2 should be used for seedlings and No. 2 for rooted cuttings. No. 3 is for mature plants needing a rich mixture.

Seedlings are usually 'pricked out' (moved) into seed trays, where they are spaced so that each has plenty of room to grow. When dealing with tomatoes and the larger type of seedling, it is much better to put them directly into small pots. If you use a peat pot it can be planted along with the plant when the time comes; this avoids any check to the plants which might result from root disturbance.

Before you prick out into trays, fill them in exactly the same way as for sowing. A small hole should then be made with a dibber and the roots of the seedling fed into it before being gently firmed into place. Once the tray is full (five rows of seven plants is convenient), the seedlings should be given a good soaking and put back on a shelf or on the staging where there is plenty of light.

If pots are used instead, exactly the same routine is followed except for rooted cuttings and seedlings with a large root system. With these, a little compost is best placed in the pot and gently firmed, then the young plant held in the pot and compost poured around the roots. When the pot is full, the compost can be lightly firmed around the plant and then watered.

POTTING ON
This is the term applied to the job of moving any plant from one pot into a larger one. The stage at which you should pot on can easily be judged by tipping the plant out of its pot and examining the roots; if they are congested and hardly any compost can be seen, the plant needs a larger pot. If, however, there is still plenty of room for

growth, leave well alone and have another look in a couple of weeks or so. Plants should only be moved into larger pots during the growing season, never in the late autumn or during the winter.

When selecting a larger pot, choose a size that will accommodate the plant for at least another month, but avoid one too big otherwise much of the fertilizer will have drained from the compost before the roots have made use of it. As a rule, go for a size that will leave a gap of about 1 cm (½ inch) all round between the inside and the root-ball of the plant. In practice, this will mean moving a plant from a 7.5 cm (3 inch) pot into a 10 cm (4 inch) one or from a 9 cm (3½ inch) one into a 13 cm (5 inch).

If the plant has a crock in the bottom of the root-ball, remove this before potting on, otherwise root growth could be impeded. When placing compost around the roots in the new pot, firm it gently as you proceed so that no air spaces are left; gentle firming is particularly important with soil-less composts, since they can easily become too compacted.

WATERING
Incorrect watering almost certainly causes more losses amongst plants than any other single reason.

During the growing season (about March to September in the greenhouse), plants will use an enormous amount of water and this should be freely available. Something like 90 per cent is transpired through the leaves to help keep the plant cool. Semi-automatic systems are, of course, particularly useful during this period as they ensure that the plants have all they need, at the same time maintaining a moist atmosphere around them. Even cacti and succulents like plenty of water; it is just that they have adapted to doing without it.

However, this need for water has to be considered with the equally important need for air around the roots – which is why drainage should always be good. If it is not, the air will be forced out of the compost and waterlogging will occur, which often results in the plant dying.

A completely different situation exists in the winter. Because there is much less natural light and a considerably lower temperature, plants should be encouraged to 'rest'. This will reduce their water needs to a minimum, and giving

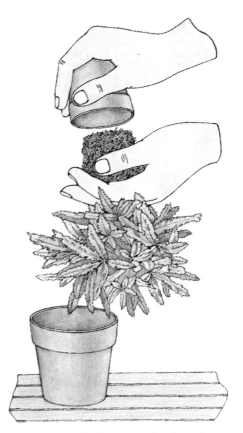

A plant is ready for a larger pot when the roots are becoming crowded.

them summer quantities is asking for trouble. As with all aspects of gardening there are exceptions, but normally the compost in the pots should be kept only just short of dry; just aim to keep the plants from wilting. They will be far healthier if kept like this.

The most common symptom of overwatering in winter is the yellowing, wilting and perhaps loss, of the lower leaves.

FEEDING
This section deals with decorative plants only. Advice on feeding fruits and vegetables will be found in the relative entry in the A-Z sections.

In many respects feeding is closely allied to watering, and is essentially a spring and summer job. You should only feed plants when they

27

are growing; it is then that they will be able to use nutrients.

It is not possible to say exactly when feeding should start in the spring, but the normal time is when you see the plants show signs of beginning to grow again. At that point, watering can be increased a little and fertilizer should be given to ensure that growth is strong and healthy. The frequency of feeding should be in line with the manufacturer's instructions on whichever make you buy. By September or October feeding should be gradually decreased and then stopped altogether until spring.

There are many different brands of fertilizer suitable for greenhouse plants, but all leading makes are likely to be completely satisfactory. They do, however, come in several different forms. The most common is the concentrated liquid type that has to be diluted before use, but you can also buy crystals that have to be dissolved. Some liquid concentrates can be applied direct to the compost a drop or two at a time, and there are granular fertilizers that are sprinkled on to the surface of the compost, fertilizer spikes which are pushed into it, and even pills that you bury amongst the roots. All of them work, and it is really a question of personal preference as to which you buy. Slow-release spikes and granules mean less frequent – but probably more expensive – feeding.

Plants grown for their foliage do best with a fertilizer with more nitrogen than potash in it; so do young flowering plants. However, once the latter start to develop flower buds, they respond better to a feed higher in potash, such as a tomato fertilizer. The composition of every fertilizer will be found on the label or carton.

PEST AND DISEASE CONTROL

One of the most disheartening things in gardening is to spend time and effort in growing plants only to find that they fall victim to some dreadful pest or disease.

A lot can be done to counteract this by growing strong plants, by being very careful not to import any 'nasties' with new plants, and by keeping a neat and clean greenhouse with no dead leaves lying about or weeds growing under the staging. Pick dead leaves or flowers off plants, and generally try to keep the greenhouse clean.

In spite of every precaution, trouble is more

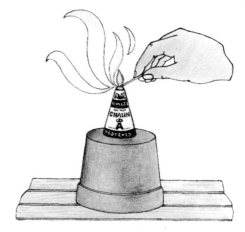

A smoke cone is one effective control method.

or less bound to strike eventually, but you can usually control the problem by prompt action:
• Always be on the look-out for the first signs of pests and diseases.
• Take action as soon as you see any.
• Identify the trouble.
• Use the correct treatment.
• Be ready to treat again if one application is insufficient.

The first two steps are straightforward enough but it may not always be easy to identify the pest or disease – this is where some of the charts produced by chemical manufacturers can be of great value. Correct identification is important for appropriate treatment.

Along with using the right material comes the need to choose the correct formulation (spray, dust, aerosol, or smoke) because some are more effective than others. In a greenhouse, fumigation with smoke or a proper greenhouse aerosol is usually best as the smoke or vapour is carried into every nook and cranny and amongst all the plants, thus ensuring that nothing remains untreated.

To control difficult pests, such as whitefly, you must be prepared to repeat the treatment.

The chart opposite will tell you which chemical to use. These are the common chemical names, which will always be on the container, but sometimes in small print.

The chemicals mentioned do not form a complete list of those that will do the job. A longer list might give you more choice, but not necessarily control the pest or disease any better. The choice of chemical is always a personal one.

PEST AND DISEASE CONTROL CHART		
Pest	**Common chemical name**	**Formulation**
Ants	borax	liquid
	sodium tetraborate	liquid
Aphids	dimethoate	spray
(greenfly,	gamma-HCH	smoke
blackfly)	malathion	aerosol
	permethrin and heptenophos	spray
	pirimiphos-methyl and	
	synergized pyrethrins	aerosol
Aphids, root	malathion	spray, used as drench
Caterpillars	permethrin	spray
	permethrin and heptenophos	spray
Earwigs	permethrin and heptenophos	spray
	gamma-HCH	dust
Leaf miners	gamma-HCH	smoke or spray
	permethrin and heptenophos	spray
	pirimiphos-methyl	spray
Mealy bugs	dimethoate	spray
	permethrin and heptenophos	spray
	pirimiphos-methyl	spray
Mealy bugs, root	dimethoate	spray, used as drench
	malathion	spray, used as drench
Red spider mites	dimethoate	spray
	pirimiphos-methyl	smoke or spray
Scale insects	dimethoate	spray
	permethrin and heptenophos	spray
Sciarid	malathion	aerosol, or spray
(fungus gnat)		used as drench
	pirimiphos-methyl	smoke
Thrips	gamma-HCH	smoke or spray
	malathion	spray
	pyrethrum and resmethrin	spray
Whitefly	bioresmethrin	aerosol or spray
	permethrin	smoke or spray
Botrytis	benomyl	spray
(grey mould)	tecnazene*	smoke
Damping off	copper compound	spray, used as drench
(in seedlings)	copper sulphate and ammonium	spray, used as drench
	carbonate (Cheshunt compound)	
Leaf spot	benomyl	spray
	mancozeb	spray
Mildew	benomyl	spray
	bupirimate and triforine	spray
	thiophanate-methyl	spray

*sold in a formulation containing
gamma-HCH insecticide

FOLIAGE PLANTS

Most foliage plants require warmth during the winter months. For this reason large formal collections of foliage plants are more frequently grown within homes, rather than in greenhouses.

The choice of varieties that will tolerate low temperatures without any artificial heat is unfortunately very limited. If you are keen to grow a range of foliage plants in the greenhouse but wish to avoid fuel costs, then a good compromise might be to supplement your collection with more interesting varieties as the weather improves.

However, should you choose to heat the greenhouse during winter, foliage plants will enable you to make full use of all available space. Some plants such as ferns and palms prefer much lower light intensities than others and, in this respect, can be grown under the staging. Remember that even if your greenhouse is heated over the winter it is advisable to raise the plants up from the ground, where temperatures are likely to be quite a bit lower than on the staging.

Unless you intend to specialize in foliage plants and are prepared to heat the greenhouse through the colder months of the year, you may well decide to use your greenhouse for other types of plants which are more economical to grow.

AGAVE*
If you have a large greenhouse, an agave can make a useful addition. It is a succulent with sharp pointed tips to its leaves. *Agave americana*, the species usually grown, can reach a height of 1.2 metres (4 ft) with a similar spread. There are several varieties with plain green or variegated leaves.
General Care: One of the great things about agaves is that they are quite hardy, tolerating high and low temperatures. They do however need lots of light. Grow them in 25-30 cm (10-12 inch) pots of John Innes No. 2 potting compost. Water agaves reasonably often during the summer, allowing the compost to become dry between waterings. During the winter, keep them quite dry. Most species can tolerate temperatures as low as 4°C (40°F).

Although grown primarily for their leaves, agaves also produce tall spikes of yellow-green flowers from the centre of the rosette of leaves in late summer. After flowering, the plant then produces offsets around the base and usually dies.
Propagation: When the mother plant has produced offsets, carefully remove them in spring or summer, potting them up singly in a 13 cm (5 inch) pot in John Innes No. 2 potting compost.

Plants can also be propagated from seeds. Sow them in April, at about 20°C (68°F), in a mixture of 4 parts seed compost to 1 part fine sand.
Pests and Diseases: Mealy bugs and root mealy bugs occasionally trouble the plant but are easily dealt with.

ALOE*
Aloes are attractive succulents with different leaf patterns formed on a rosette of leaves in an overlapping arrangement. They form flower spikes in spring. Although the flowers are not very large, they are none the less attractive and vary in colour from yellow to orange, pink and red.

One of the most hardy and successful varieties that can be grown under glass is the popular *Aloe variegata* or partridge-breasted aloe, which has green-and-white-striped fleshy leaves and produces pinkish-orange flowers on 30 cm (12 inch) flower spikes.
General Care: Aloes are relatively hardy and adaptable and, although they prefer a well-lit situation, they can tolerate a slightly shaded position. During the spring and summer, water regularly, but not excessively, allowing the plant to dry out in between waterings. In the winter, however, the plant must be kept on the dry side, when it will tolerate temperatures down to around 4°C (40°F). Grow in John Innes No. 2 potting compost and in suitable sized pots up to 30 cm (12

Agave americana marginata

2 metres (5-6½ ft) with a diameter of about 1 metre (3 ft). Although it is related to the monkey puzzle tree which is grown outside in the garden, *Auraucaria excelsa* will not tolerate frost.

General Care: The araucaria adapts to a wide range of conditions from shade to full sun and at temperatures down to 10°C (50°F). During the spring and summer, try to allow the plant to dry out in between waterings and in the winter water infrequently, keeping the compost on the dry side. Grow it in John Innes No. 2 potting compost in 20-25 cm (8-10 inch) pots.

Propagation: The Norfolk Island pine should be propagated from seed sown in March in half or dwarf pots filled with John Innes No. 1 potting compost. Sprinkle the seed on the compost and lightly cover with more compost. Then keep the compost moist and warm at around 20°C (68°F) until the seeds have germinated. Grow on in the pots until large enough to handle then pot them up singly in 9 cm (3½ inch) pots filled with John Innes No. 2 potting compost.

Araucaria may also be propagated from cuttings in spring. Take 7.5 cm (3 inches) shoots and insert in a mixture of equal parts of peat and sand at a temperature of 13-16°C (55-61°F). When rooted, pot up as for seedlings.

Pests and Diseases: Usually trouble-free, but occasionally araucaria is troubled by mealy bugs and root mealy bugs.

inches) as the plant gets larger. **Propagation:** It is quite easy to propagate aloes. They can be grown from offsets separated carefully from the mother plant in summer and potted up singly in 9 cm (3½ inch) pots containing a peat and sand potting compost.

Aloes can also be raised from seed sown in March in a medium of 4 parts seed compost to 1 part fine sand and kept at around 20°C (68°F). When the seedlings are large enough to handle, prick out and pot them up separately in a similar mixture.

Pests and Diseases: Mealy bugs and root mealy bugs are the most usual pests.

ARAUCARIA*

The variety commonly grown is *Araucaria excelsa*, the Norfolk Island pine, which resembles a soft feathery Christmas tree with radiating branches of dark green 'needles'. It grows to a height of around 1.5-

ASPARAGUS FERN *

There are several different plants known as asparagus fern, but none of them is a true fern. Two varieties in particular are usually grown as pot plants under glass – *Asparagus plumosus* and *Asparagus sprengeri*.

General Care: Asparagus fern is very easy to grow. It should be kept in a well-lit position, but shaded from direct sunlight in summer. Grow it in 13 cm (5 inch) pots of John Innes No. 3 potting compost or a soil-less compost, and water frequently in summer. Conversely, keep it on the dry side in winter, and aim for a minimum temperature of about 10°C (50°F).

Asparagus fern can be grown on the staging or under it, in the border, or in a hanging basket if you are short of

Asparagus sprengeri (asparagus fern)

space. Whichever way you grow it, this plant will provide you with feathery foliage that can be used in floral arrangements. It will be necessary to feed with a high nitrogen fertilizer if the foliage is cut frequently.

Propagation: This is very easy – the plants are simply divided in spring. Moisten the compost well and gently tease apart the root, using a knife to cut through some of the fibrous root growth. Pot up each division into a pot filled with potting compost and grow on.

Pests and Diseases: Asparagus ferns can sometimes be attacked by mealy bugs and root mealy bugs, and occasionally by scale insects.

ASPIDISTRA *

Aspidistras, with their broad dark green or variegated leaves, take up little room in a greenhouse because of their erect habit. They reach a height of 30 cm (12 inches) and, although not outstandingly attractive, can complement a collection of foliage plants grown under glass.

General Care: Aspidistras should not be grown in direct sunlight as this can scorch the leaves. They are best in a slightly shaded situation in a corner or perhaps even under the staging in the greenhouse. A humid environment is appreciated and for this reason, aspidistras often thrive better under glass than when grown indoors.

Do not overwater and allow the compost to get on the dry side in between waterings. In winter, it is essential to avoid overwatering, because aspidistras will rot if kept too wet at low temperatures: aim for a minimum temperature of around 10°C (50°F). Grow in 15-25 cm (6-10 inch) pots of John Innes No. 2 potting compost. Feed monthly during summer with a diluted liquid fertilizer.

Propagation: The best way to propagate aspidistra is to divide the plant carefully in spring or summer. Moisten the compost and then use a sharp knife to separate the plant into the appropriate number of pieces, potting each up singly in 13 cm (5 inch) pots of potting compost.

Pests and Diseases: Red spider mites, mealy bugs and root mealy bugs will attack aspidistras. Red spider mite can be a particular nuisance.

ASPLENIUM*

Commonly known as the bird's nest fern, the *Asplenium nidus avis* is a fairly tough fern with broad fronds that lack the usual finely cut appearance of other ferns. The fronds are shiny and are bright green in colour, growing up to about 1 metre (3 ft) on mature specimens.

General Care: In common with other ferns, aspleniums are happiest when out of direct sunlight as it bleaches the fronds. Probably one of the best places to grow them is under the staging, where they will thrive particularly if planted directly into the greenhouse border. Keep the compost relatively moist all through the year, but in the winter keep it slightly drier. If possible avoid overhead watering. During the winter, aspleniums will happily tolerate temperatures down to around 10°C (50°F) and sometimes even lower. Grow them in 13 cm (5 inch) pots of peat-based compost.

Propagation: As the plants get older, they will produce dark brown, gill-like growths on the underside of some of the fronds. The spores produced from these can be collected by tapping the particular fronds over a sheet of paper. The spores appear as brown dust and these can be sown in summer on to the surface of a half pot filled with a mixture of equal parts peat and a loam-based seed compost, or a peat-based seed compost. This should be kept moist and covered with a polythene bag to conserve humidity until the spores germinate. When the plantlets are large enough to handle, gently prick out and pot up singly in potting compost in 9 cm (3½ inch) pots.

Pests and Diseases: Scale insects are a particular nuisance to asplenium, and will attack both upper and lower surfaces of the fronds.

BEGONIA REX**

Begonia rex is one of the most beautiful foliage begonias, having roughly heart-shaped leaves in a wide range of colours and patterns.

General Care: This begonia likes a well-lit position away from strong direct sun. It will grow quite happily beneath the staging. The plant is fairly

Aspidistra

General Care: Chlorophytums are equally happy in pots, hanging baskets or troughs, but look particularly effective growing in hanging baskets. During the spring and summer, keep them in full light and water frequently, but avoid allowing the plants to become too wet. In the winter keep them on the dry side, and they will quite happily tolerate temperatures down to around 10°C (50°F) or lower. When the roots really fill the pot, pot on until they are in 20 cm (8 inch) pots, and feed weekly in summer with liquid fertilizer. Use either a John Innes or a soilless compost.

Propagation: The plant produces its characteristic flowering trails in spring and summer and you can propagate from the little plantlets when they have grown a little and you can see the roots starting to form. Either place them lightly in 9 cm (3½ inch) pots filled with potting compost whilst still attached to the trails or, if you are feeling bold, cut them off and take a chance! Although the former almost guarantees success, the latter rarely fails. Once you have separated the plantlets from the mother plant, trim back the trails to keep the main plant looking tidy.

Pests and Diseases: Aphids can attack chlorophytum during the spring and summer. Mealy bugs and root mealy bugs are sometimes troublesome.

tolerant of a warm, dry environment and prefers a temperature of about 18°C (65°F), though a winter temperature of 10°C (50°F) is adequate if the compost is kept fairly dry.

Propagation: Select a well-formed, mature (not old) leaf, lay it face down and cut it into postage-stamp squares using a sharp knife. Lightly dip the underside of the leaf cuttings in hormone rooting powder and gently lay right-side up on the surface of a seed tray or half pot filled with moistened seed compost. Cover with a polythene bag and keep at about 21°C (70°F). Remove any cuttings that wither or rot and take off the polythene when the little plantlets start

to grow. When they are large enough to handle, gently prick them out and pot up.

Pests and Diseases: Mildew and grey mould (botrytis) may occasionally infect the plant. Mealy bugs also sometimes attack begonias.

CHLOROPHYTUM*

The spider plant, *Chlorophytum comosum*, also called the St Bernard lily, is one of the most common plants grown, with its green and white variegated leaves and long trailing runners. Although the chlorophytum grows reasonably well as a houseplant, it is happier in a greenhouse, where, with the advantage of better conditions, its habit and colour really excel.

COLEUS*

Coleus, commonly called flame nettles, are super little plants to raise and grow under glass. They are available in a very wide range of highly coloured leaf forms. Apart from providing a wealth of colour in the greenhouse, they can also be used as summer bedding plants or as houseplants. They are only likely to succeed as bedding plants in a sheltered position in favourable areas.

General Care: Coleus should be allowed as much light as possible; lack of light will cause the growth to stretch and lose its colour. As the plant grows, pinch out the top shoot or shoots from time to time to encourage a compact and well-shaped plant. Insignificant flowers will be produced and these can be pinched out to maintain the plant's vigour.

Water coleus freely in summer, but keep on the dry side in winter. Feed mature plants regularly. A temperature of about 10°C (50°F) should be sufficient to see the plants through winter, although they do tend to become rather

straggly if kept too long. Grow coleus in 13 cm (5 inch) pots of John Innes No. 3 potting compost, or a soil-less compost.

Propagation: Coleus can be propagated from seed in early spring. Sow seeds in half pots, dwarf pots or seed trays filled with seed compost, and keep at around 18°C (65°F). When large enough to handle, prick out the seedlings and pot up singly in 9 cm (3½ inch) pots of potting compost.

Coleus can also be propagated from cuttings taken during July, August and even into September. These cuttings can be obtained when you trim the plant to encourage a bushy shape. Dip the cuttings in hormone rooting powder and insert, one to a pot, in 9 cm (3½ inch) pots of John Innes No. 1 potting compost, keeping them moist and at a temperature of about 18°C (65°F) until rooted.

Pests and Diseases: Coleus may be attacked by aphids.

CYPERUS*

Cyperus alternifolius is a delicate looking reed-like plant with slender shoots up to 1 metre (3 ft) high and umbrella-like 'fronds' at the top. The attractive bright green foliage makes the plant a useful foil to a mixed plant display.

General Care: Cyperus are surprisingly easy to grow and break the watering rules of plant care. Unlike other plants that should be allowed to dry out a little before re-watering, cyperus prefer to be kept moist all the time. In fact, they are happiest when allowed to sit in a saucer of water continuously. During the winter, it is best not to expose the plant to temperatures below 10°C (50°F); aim for an optimum of between 13°C (55°F) and 16°C (60°F). Cyperus are fairly adaptable to the degree of light that they are exposed to, although you will achieve the best results by placing them in a lightly shaded situation.

Propagation: The best way to propagate cyperus is by division. During the spring or summer, when the plant is most tolerant of any disturbance, divide the roots with a sharp knife, potting up each piece in a suitably sized pot filled with John Innes No. 2 potting compost. Pot on into 13 cm (5 inch) pots of John Innes No. 3 potting compost, or good garden soil.

Pests and Diseases: Mealy bugs and aphids sometimes attack cyperus but can easily be dealt with.

LEFT: Coleus
OPPOSITE PAGE: Chlorophytum (spider plant)

35

ECHEVERIA*

There are many different echeveria with attractive rosettes of leaves and sprays of flowers ranging from white to yellow, orange and red. Some can be used to add a little extra interest to summer bedding with their unusual form. They are mostly only 7.5 cm (3 inches) high and often have a waxy bloom to the leaves. Flowers are produced on short stems in summer.

General Care: Echeveria are quite tough, and, as they are succulents, care should be taken not to overwater them. Care should also be taken not to splash the foliage as this will leave marks. During the spring and summer allow the plants to dry out in between waterings, and in winter keep them on the dry side. They will then be tolerant of temperatures down to around 4°C (40°F). Although fairly adaptable, they are happiest when allowed to grow in a situation of full light.

Propagation: The easiest way to propagate echeveria is gently to remove the fleshy leaves and to insert them in a mixture of seed compost and sand in a 4:1 ratio. The compost should be kept barely moist until the plants have rooted, otherwise the leaf pads may rot off.

Echeverias can also be germinated from seed in the same compost as that used for the cuttings. Fill a half pot with the compost and sow the seed on the surface. Lightly cover the seed with fine sand and keep at 20°C (68°F) until it has germinated. Grow the seedlings on until large enough to handle and, as with the young plants raised from

Fatshedera lizei

leaves, pot up in 9 cm (3½ inch) pots of John Innes No. 2 potting compost.

Pests and Diseases: Mealy bugs and root mealy bugs occasionally attack echeveria.

EUONYMUS*

The most common species of this plant, *Euonymus radicans,* is usually grown as a houseplant but it can alternatively be grown as a greenhouse shrub that requires no heat at all during the winter. The brightly coloured variegated forms can easily be grown outside, although the growth under glass is usually much more lush and vigorous.

General Care: Euonymus are very easy to grow. Avoid overwatering, and try to ensure that the plants dry out in between waterings. Although these plants are very adaptable, they should be grown in a situation of full light for the brightest variegation of the foliage. There is no need to worry about low winter temperatures, euonymus will even tolerate frost.

Grow in John Innes No. 2 potting compost in 13-25 cm (5-10 inch) pots, or until they become too large for your greenhouse. You can then plant them out in a sheltered part of the garden.

Propagation: Euonymus can easily be propagated from shoot cuttings, about 7.5 cm (3 inches) long, in August. Dip the cutting into hormone rooting powder and insert approximately three cuttings in a 9 cm (3½ inch) pot of seed compost. Cover them with a polythene bag to conserve moisture and avoid leaf dehydration. When the cuttings have rooted, remove the polythene bag and grow on.

Pests and Diseases: Aphids, mealy bugs, caterpillars and red spider mites will attack the plant, particularly during the spring and summer.

FATSHEDERA*

The deep green 'five-fingered' leaves of the *fatshedera lizei* provide an interesting shape in a foliage greenhouse plant collection. The plant climbs readily and will reach a height of 1.2-2.4 metres (4-8 ft).

General Care: Fatshedera is quite tough and capable of withstanding temperatures down to around 7°C (45°F) over winter. It should, however, be kept on the dry side and watered infrequently. During the summer, give the plant a slightly shaded situation away from direct sunlight, otherwise the leaves tend to lose their deep green colour. It should be allowed to dry out in between waterings, as it is sometimes prone to root rot. Grow it in 15-20 cm (6-8 inch) pots of John Innes No. 2 potting compost.

Propagation: Fatshedera can be propagated in July and August from tip cuttings, about 7.5 cm (3 inches) long, or stem cuttings with a leaf and a section of stem about 1 cm (½ inch) above the leaf and about 2.5 cm (1 inch) below. In either case, dip the bottom of the stem into hormone rooting powder and insert three cuttings in a 9 cm (3½ inch) pot of potting compost. Cover with a polythene bag to reduce water loss from the leaves; remove this when the cuttings have rooted and leave them to grow on in the same pot.

Pests and Diseases: Fatshedera is occasionally subject to attack by red spider mites, aphids, mealy bugs and root mealy bugs.

FICUS PUMILA*

The diminutive *Ficus pumila* or creeping fig is an ideal plant to grow under the staging in a greenhouse, either in pots, in a basket suspended from the staging or any other type of container placed out of direct light. The trailing or climbing habit of the plant is enhanced by its small, heart-shaped leaves that quickly hide any support canes. It reaches a height of 15-20 cm (6-8 inches).

General Care: Provided you do not allow *Ficus pumila* to dry out, you should have no problems in successfully growing the plant. As well as keeping the compost moist, take care to ensure that the plant is kept out of sunlight. Damping down the greenhouse is helpful in summer.

During the winter months, *Ficus pumila* will happily tolerate temperatures down to 10°C (50°F). Grow it in 10 cm (4 inch) pots of John Innes No. 2 potting compost, or a soil-less compost. Pot on into larger pots as necessary.

Propagation: As the plant grows, it will become necessary to trim it. From April to June, you can use the trimmings for cuttings. Cut the lengths into pieces about

Ficus pumila

7.5 cm (3 inches) long and dip into hormone rooting powder, then insert about five of them into a 9 cm (3½ inch) pot filled with seed compost. To avoid leaf dehydration, cover the pot with a polythene bag and then keep at around 18°C (65°F) until the cuttings have rooted. Grow on in the pot, removing the polythene bag when the plants appear to be growing.

Pests and Diseases: *Ficus pumila* is occasionally subject to attack by aphids, mealy bugs and root mealy bugs.

FICUS ELASTICA*

The rubber plant will happily grow in your greenhouse provided you can give it enough head-room. Under such ideal conditions, the bold, oval-leaved plant may eventually grow so well that you will have to prune it each year to keep it in check.

General Care: The rubber plant is very hardy and adaptable and, although it prefers a lightly shaded situation, it will grow well in full light. Try to allow the compost to dry out between waterings. In winter, the *Ficus elastica* will tolerate temperatures down to around 10°C (50°F), provided the compost is on the dry side, but it prefers temperatures in the region of 16-18°C (61-65°F). Start in 10 cm (4 inch) pots of John Innes No. 2 potting compost or a soil-less compost. Pot on in April until the plant is in a 30 cm (12 inch) pot.

Propagation: *Ficus elastica* is a very difficult plant to propagate from cuttings, but is worth a try next time you decide to trim back the plant in late spring. Cut up the stem into pieces about 5 cm (2 inches) long with a leaf in the middle. Dip the bottom 2.5 cm (1 inch) of the stem into hormone rooting powder and insert in a 9 cm (3½ inch) pot of seed compost, rolling the leaf loosely around a cane for support and placing a rubber band around the leaf and cane to secure it. Keep the cutting at a temperature of 27°C (80°F) until rooted, which may be six to eight weeks.

You can also take ordinary stem cuttings, which you may find easier. This method is usually more successful, unless you are trying to propagate a large number of new plants.

Pests and Diseases: Aphids, mealy bugs and scale insects can cause problems.

GYNURA*

Gynura, or the velvet nettle, is a low-growing trailing plant with fleshy foliage, which has a violet-coloured sheen.

General Care: Gynuras like a fairly well-lit situation as this helps to brighten the coloration of the leaves, but they also need to be shaded from hot sun

in summer. Grow in 13 cm

Ficus elastica (rubber plant)

(5 inch) pots of John Innes potting compost No. 2, or a soil-less compost. To avoid overwatering the plants in summer allow the compost to become slightly dry before re-watering, but keep the atmosphere moist by damping down the greenhouse. During the winter, do not allow the temperature to drop below 10°C (50°F) and keep the compost a little drier to avoid root rot.

Although they are by nature trailing plants, gynuras can also climb to about 1 metre (3 ft) if given the support of a cane – but do not expect too much of them!

To keep the leaf colour, it helps to pinch out the orange-yellow tiny dandelion-like flowers. Don't be tempted to leave the flowers until they open, as they might look interesting, but smell horrid!

Propagation: Gynuras are easy to propagate in spring. Simply pinch off pieces, about 7.5 cm (3 inches) long, and dip the bottom of each stem into hormone rooting powder before inserting about three cuttings into a 9 cm (3½ inch) pot containing a mixture of equal parts peat and sand. When rooted, pot up singly in 9 cm (3½ inch) pots of John Innes No. 1 potting compost. Gynuras are best propagated afresh every two years.

Pests and Diseases: Mealy bugs, root mealy bugs and aphids may attack gynura from to time.

MONSTERA*

Monstera deliciosa, the Swiss cheese plant, can make a useful greenhouse plant, if you can accommodate it, for it

Monstera (Swiss cheese plant)

grows up to 2 metres (6½ ft) high, and its large leaves, with their characteristic holes and slits, may soon swamp the other plants in your collection. It has numerous aerial roots which can be trained down into the pot or left to dangle from the stems.

General Care: Monstera prefers a lightly shaded situation with a minimum winter temperature of about 10°C (50°F). During the spring and summer, the plant should be kept reasonably moist, but in winter it is preferable to keep the compost on the dry side to avoid the roots rotting. Grow it in John Innes No. 3 potting compost, and pot on annually until in 30 cm (12 inch) pots. Feed every two weeks in summer with weak liquid fertilizer. Fortunately, the usual humid conditions of a greenhouse help to maintain the characteristic slits in the leaves, unlike the normal household environment where the leaves sometimes revert to plain heart-shape.

Propagation: *Monstera deliciosa* can be propagated from side shoots that are teased away from the mother plant when they are about 15 cm (6 inches) tall and potted up on their own in a 13 cm (5 inch) pot of John Innes No. 3 potting compost. However, the best way to raise monstera is from seed. If you can obtain seeds, sow in a pot of seed compost at about 21°C (70°F), potting the seedlings up singly in potting compost when large enough to handle.

Pests and Diseases: Monstera is sometimes attacked by aphids, mealy bugs, root mealy bugs and scale insects, but is generally free from pests.

39

Peperomia magnoliaefolia

PEPEROMIA MAGNOLIAEFOLIA*

This plant, more commonly known as the desert privet, is a tough plant to include in your collection of greenhouse plants. It has brightly variegated yellow and green fleshy round leaves, and grows to a height of 15 cm (6 inches).

General Care: *Peperomia magnoliaefolia* is very easy to grow in a well-lit position in the greenhouse. It takes up little space when grown on the staging and can also grow well in a hanging basket. Keep it in small pots up to 9 cm (3½ inches), using John Innes No. 1 potting compost, or a soil-less compost. Keep the plant on the dry side, watering infrequently during the winter as the plant is more likely to survive the lower temperatures if it is dry at the roots. Even so, avoid temperatures below 10°C (50°F).

Propagation: When the desert privet becomes rather straggly, it is a good time to think about propagating it. In summer, cut off the top growth in pieces about 7.5 cm (3 inches) long and, after dipping in hormone rooting powder, insert about three cuttings into a 9 cm (3½ inch) pot of seed compost. Covering the pot with polythene is unnecessary and can cause the cuttings to rot. Pot up the rooted cuttings singly.

Pests and Diseases: Aphids and red spider mites sometimes attack, especially during spring and summer.

PHILODENDRON SCANDENS*

This is the sweetheart plant and has heart-shaped dark green leaves which grace its climbing or semi-trailing stems. It provides a useful background plant to set off the brighter plants in your display. It can grow up to about 2 metres (6 ft) high.

General Care: *Philodendron scandens* prefers a slightly shaded situation and can even grow quite happily under the staging in a pot, or in a hanging basket where, if allowed to do so, it will trail over the pot as well as climbing up any support that you can give it.

To avoid overwatering the plant, keep just moist in between waterings. In particular keep the plant on the dry side in winter to avoid any chance of root rot. The sweetheart plant can tolerate winter temperatures of 10°C (50°F). Plant it in soil-less compost in a 15 cm (6 inch) pot, potting on every other year until in a 25 cm (10 inch) pot.

Propagation: In time the plant may become rather leggy and replacement plants should be propagated from it in May or June. Trim back wayward growth and cut into pieces of stem with a leaf and about 2.5 cm (1 inch) of stem above and below the leaf. Dip the bottom piece of stem into hormone rooting powder and insert between three and five in a 9 cm (3 inch) pot of peat-based seed compost. Once rooted, the cuttings can be left in the pot to grow on, making a more compact, better-formed plant.

Pests and Diseases: Mealy bugs, root mealy bugs and, to a lesser extent, aphids and red spider mites, may sometimes infect the sweetheart plant, but it is not often attacked.

PILEA CADIEREI*

Pilea cadierei, perhaps better known as the aluminium plant, has crinkly grey and green, slightly pointed oval leaves. It grows up to about 30 cm (12 inches) and will complement the brighter plants of your collection.

General Care: Although the aluminium plant is easy to

keep, it does have a few likes and dislikes. It prefers light shade, so avoid direct sunlight as this could cause leaf-yellowing or scorching. Take care with watering, as the plant can be overwatered fairly easily even though during the summer months it prefers a reasonably moist situation. In winter the plant should be kept on the dry side and watered far less frequently.

A minimum winter temperature of about 10°C (50°F) is required, though the plant will be more tolerant of low temperatures provided that it is not wet at the roots. Grow it in 13 cm (5 inch) pots of John Innes No. 2 potting compost,

or a soil-less compost. Feed every two weeks in summer with weak liquid fertilizer.

Propagation: The aluminium plant is very easy to propagate. Simply cut or pinch off shoots about 5-7.5 cm (2-3 inches) long, dip into hormone rooting powder and insert about five cuttings to a 9 cm (3½ inch) pot of potting compost. Rooting is fairly rapid and should take only about two to three weeks during the spring and summer. Pinching out the tips of the shoots also helps to encourage a compact and better-formed shape.

Pests and Diseases: Aphids, mealy bugs and root mealy bugs sometimes attack.

PITTOSPORUM*

The pittosporum is an attractive evergreen shrub with glossy leaves, sometimes grown outside in favourable areas. It is not very hardy and is normally killed by the frost, but it does, however, make a good greenhouse plant, provided you can afford the room. Its foliage is very popular with flower arrangers. There are plain green and variegated forms.

General Care: Pittosporum likes a very well-lit situation to bring out the best in the colour of its leaves. Keep the compost moderately moist but do not overwater. In the winter, keep the compost drier and the plant will then tolerate temperatures down to around 7°C (45°F). It can be grown in good garden soil or John Innes No. 2 potting compost. Trim the plant to maintain its shape and to keep it compact.

Propagation: Cuttings about 7.5-10 cm (3-4 inches) long may be taken in mid-summer. Use semi-mature side shoots that are neither woody nor tender and fleshy. Dip the cuttings into hormone rooting powder and then insert singly into 9 cm (3½ inch) pots of seed compost. Keep at around 20°C (68°F) until rooted and grow on until the root system is well formed. It is probably better to leave the plants in these pots until the following spring when they should be potted into 13 cm (5 inch) pots of potting compost.

Pests and Diseases: Pittosporum is not normally troubled by pests or diseases.

Pilea cadierei (aluminium plant)

Platycerium bifurcatum (stag's horn fern)

enough to handle into 9 cm (3½ inch) pots in a similar compost.

Pests and Diseases: Scale insects are the most likely problem.

SANSEVIERIA*
The mother-in-law's tongue, or *Sansevieria trifasciata* 'Laurentii', is a very hardy succulent that takes up little room and yet provides a colourful addition to your collection. It grows about 50 cm (20 inches) tall and has bold, green and yellow striped leaves. During the summer, the plant may produce a spike of greenish-white fragrant flowers.

General Care: Mother-in-law's tongue loves sunlight and is happiest in a well-lit situation in the greenhouse. Although easy to keep, do take care with watering, for the plant is relatively easy to overwater. Allow the plant to dry out completely between waterings.

During the winter, the plant should be kept almost completely dry; water it only if you maintain a temperature around 13°C (55°F) or to avoid dehydration. Otherwise the sansevieria will tolerate temperatures down to 10°C (50°F). Grow it in 13 cm (5 inch) pots of soil-less compost or John Innes No. 2 potting compost. Feed monthly in summer with weak liquid fertilizer.

Propagation: Propagate the plant by using offsets when they are at least 10 cm (4 inches) tall. To do this, mois-

PLATYCERIUM*
Perhaps better known as the stag's horn fern, *Platycerium bifurcatum* is an unusual fern with fronds that look just like the antlers of a stag. It is a tree-living fern, and ideal to grow in a hanging basket or wired to a piece of cork bark filled with compost. It can, however, be grown just as easily under the staging. It grows to a height of 45-75 cm (1½-2½ ft), with a similar spread.

General Care: Platyceriums are very adaptable and, unlike most other ferns, will tolerate a higher light intensity, although a slightly shaded situation is best.

Allow the compost to dry out a little in between waterings and certainly keep it drier during the winter than in the summer. In the winter, avoid

temperatures lower than 10°C (50°F). It is best grown in a compost of 2 parts fibrous peat, 1 part spagnum moss and 1 part fibrous loam. Good drainage is essential.

Propagation: Platycerium can be propagated from the spores that are released from the brown patches on the underside of mature frond tips. When these tips are visible, and become darker and more pronounced, tap the frond over a sheet of paper. The spores, once collected, look like fine dust and can be sown on the surface of a half pot filled with a mixture of equal parts peat and loam-based seed compost, or in a peat-based seed compost. Place the pot in a polythene bag and keep at about 21°C (70°F) until the spores have germinated. Pot on singly when large ten the compost and tease apart the small plant, using a sharp knife to sever any stubborn connections. Pot up the pieces either singly or together to make a more compact-looking plant, using potting compost. Do take care, though, not to use too large a pot, and be extra careful with watering for the first few weeks after potting up the cuttings.

You can also root leaf cuttings. Cut a leaf into 5 cm (2 inch) sections and insert them – right way up – in moist potting compost. Pot up once they have rooted.

Pests and Diseases: Sansevieria usually remains free from pests, although the flowers can sometimes be attacked by aphids.

TRADESCANTIA*

The tradescantia is an attractive trailing plant that is available in several variegated forms with cream, green or purple leaves. Unfortunately, it does tend to become rather leggy with age and is better as a young plant.

General Care: Tradescantias can be grown in a number of ways, either as pot plants in their own right on the staging amongst the rest of your plants or as hanging basket subjects. Whatever you decide to do, be sure to give them as much light as possible, otherwise the colours will dull and the leaves will become very green.

Water freely in summer, but keep them just moist in winter, at a temperature of 10°C (50°F). Either grow in John Innes No. 2 potting compost, or a soil-less compost.

As a tradescantia gets older, it becomes leggy, with stems devoid of leaves. Any new lush growth is generally well away from the pot, which gives the plant an untidy appearance. Keep it pinched back to encourage bushiness, and remove shoots that lose their variegation.

Propagation: When the plant becomes leggy, trim it back, taking each shoot as a cutting. Each cutting should be trimmed to a length of about 5 cm (2 inches) before being inserted, three or five to a 9 cm (3½ inch) pot, in John Innes No. 1 potting compost. Rooting should take only about two or three weeks and the plants can be left to grow on in the same pot, where they will form compact, well-balanced plants.

Pests and Diseases: Tradescantia is rarely troubled by pests, which makes it one of the easiest plants to grow.

Sanseviera (mother-in-law's tongue)

FLOWERING PLANTS

There is nothing quite like a greenhouse full of flowering plants, providing a feast of colour and splendour throughout the year.

The greatest show occurs from spring to summer, though certain varieties, such as carnations and chrysanthemums, can be encouraged to flower throughout the year. These do, however, require special treatment, and the greenhouse needs to be heated at colder times of the year.

Even if you want to economise on heating, you can still grow astilbe, bulbs, hydrangea and polyanthus over winter for early spring flowers. Followed by fuchsia, geranium and impatiens for early summer. Begonia, cyclamen and solanum can be grown for late summer to early autumn flowering, but from October onwards they will require some warmth. If you don't want to heat the greenhouse, find a position for them in the home. Solanum produce attractive orange fruits which last over the festive Christmas season.

A greenhouse is particularly useful for promoting early flowers on plants, such as spring bulbs or polyanthus.

Flowering plants are ideal companions to fruit and vegetables, for most varieties share a liking for fairly high light intensities. To provide a decorative note throughout the year it is worth devoting some space to flowering plants even if your main priority in the greenhouse is vegetables or fruit.

AMARYLLIS*
The amaryllis, or hippeastrum, is a bold winter-flowering plant that produces up to four beautiful large flowers on a tall stem. These range in colour from white to pink and red, and each flower measures up to 10 cm (4 inches) long and across. The broad, flat leaves can grow rather long and strap-like, but the plant rarely grows more than 60 cm (2 ft) tall.

General Care: The hippeastrum should be grown in as much light as possible, otherwise it can become very leggy. To encourage it to start into growth, provide gentle heat and water sparingly until the plant is in active growth. As it starts to grow from the bulb, take care with watering, as it can be relatively easily over-watered in the first few weeks. Thereafter the plant will require increasing amounts of water, and a weekly liquid feed. After flowering the plant should be allowed to grow until the leaves begin to yellow. It should then be kept dry through the dormant period during the autumn and early winter before starting into growth again.

Pot the bulb in a 13-17 cm (5-7 inch) pot of John Innes No. 2 potting compost, leaving about one third of the bulb exposed. The bulbs need a minimum temperature of 13°C (55°F).

Propagation: Hippeastrums can be propagated from seeds or offsets. Offsets will flower sooner but are not quite so numerous. To grow them, simply separate the offsets from the plant and pot on singly.

Seedlings are more numerous, but usually take longer. Sow the seed when ripe in half pots of seed compost and germinate at about 21°C (70°F), potting up singly in potting compost in 9 cm (3½ inch) pots to begin with and finally into 13 cm (5 inch) pots. Plants raised from seed may take three years to flower.

Pests and Diseases: Mealy bugs sometimes affect the flowers of the plant.

ASTILBE*
Astilbes, sometimes called spireas, can be grown outside but, grown under glass, they will flower much earlier and provide a splash of colour in the late months of winter. The bright flower plumes vary in colour from white through pink and rose to red. They are borne on finely cut dark green foliage.

General Care: Astilbes love light and water. To get the best from the plants, grow them in the lightest situation possible in the greenhouse and water very frequently. Do not, on any account, allow the plants to dry out otherwise they will dehydrate and they may not recover. To prolong the flowering period, try to keep

Pink flowering amaryllis (Hippeastrum)

the plants at about 13-15°C (55-59°F).

When flowering is finished, if you wish, you can plant them out in the garden for the summer, bringing them back into the greenhouse about October. As astilbes are fully hardy, there is no need to worry about a minimum winter temperature. Keep them in 13 cm (5 inch) pots of John Innes potting compost No. 2.

Propagation: The best way to propagate astilbe is to divide the clumps in spring with a sharp knife, potting each piece up separately into a pot of potting compost. The crown of the plant should be left just proud of the compost surface.

Pests and Diseases: Astilbes are particularly prone to attack by aphids, which seem to enjoy not only the leaves but the flowers as well.

AZALEA**

The Indian azalea or *Rhododendron indicum* is not frost hardy, but it grows well in the greenhouse, and makes a good display during the winter months. The plant flowers in spring and comes in a wide range of colours from white through pink to salmon and red. With care the plant may last in flower from six to eight weeks.

General Care: The Indian azalea should be kept in the lightest position possible in the greenhouse with a minimum winter temperature of about 10°C (50°F). Watering is most important and on no account should the plant be allowed to dry out. Keep it in 15-20 cm (6-8 inch) pots of lime-free compost. The conditions of high humidity and high light intensities that are usual under glass help to encourage the plant to produce flowers in profusion.

After the plant has flowered, it can be placed outside from May onwards when frosts have finished, until September when the plant should be brought back under glass again. To grow the azalea outside during the summer, plunge it into a peat bed, still in its pot and keep moist throughout the summer months. Syringeing the plants with water daily from December onwards will encourage profuse flowering.

Propagation: The Indian azalea is not very easy to propagate, although it can be raised from seed or cuttings with difficulty.

Pests and Diseases: Aphids can be a particular nuisance on the flowers.

BEGONIA*

There are many different varieties of begonia that can be grown in your greenhouse. However, the large-flowered and hanging varieties that are tuberous rooted will probably give you most pleasure. The flowers of each are large and

45

highly coloured and will give a magnificent display during the summer in colours that range from white to pink, salmon, yellow, orange and red.

General Care: Whichever variety of tuberous-rooted begonia you grow, take particular care when planting and growing them for the first few weeks. The large-flowered tuberous rooted begonia can be grown in 13 cm (5 inch) pots, whereas the trailing variety can be grown in similar pots or in hanging baskets.

In February or March, light-ly fill the containers with peat-based potting compost and plant the tubers on the top, convex surface down, concave surface up. Leave the top of the tubers proud of the compost and moisten the compost. Keep the tubers at about 18°C (65°F) until the shoots start to appear. They can then be grown on at a more moderate temperature around 15°C (50°F) or lower, but do not allow the temperature to drop

Display of orange and red flowering begonias

below 10°C (50°F) otherwise the plant may rot.

Begonias like a light but slightly shaded situation, so avoid prolonged exposure to the sun. Take care to ensure that the plants do not dry out; they require a fair amount of water.

After flowering, from mid to late summer, allow the plants to die back to the tuber and then dry out the compost. Gently lift the tuber and store in dry peat over winter at a temperature of around 10°C (50°F).

Propagation: Begonias can be propagated from seed sown at around 20°C (68°F) in half pots filled with seed compost. Prick out and pot up the seedlings singly in a potting compost when large enough to handle.

Pests and Diseases: Begonias may occasionally be attacked by aphids, particularly on their flowers and buds.

BULBS*

During the winter months, it is an excellent idea to make use of your greenhouse to force spring bulbs into early growth to provide you with a feast of colour whilst the bulbs in your garden are often still buried under snow. Tulips, crocus, hyacinths, daffodils and narcissi can all be successfully grown with the minimum of care. What is more, you can use the previous year's growing bags or they can be grown in pots, troughs or any other suitable container.

General Care: Having chosen your container, fill it with a suitable compost such as John Innes No. 2 potting compost, bulb fibre or last year's growing bag compost. Plant the

bulbs in the container; hyacinths should have their top halves above the compost, whilst tulips, crocus, daffodils and narcissi are buried so that their tops are about 5 cm (2 inches) below the surface of the compost. Keep the compost moist and cover the container with a bucket or other material to keep out the light. Then simply leave until the shoots are about 5 cm (2 inches) tall. Remove the cover and expose the bulbs to full light, keeping them adequately watered. Within a matter of a few weeks, the bulbs will flower and will provide a real spectacle.

After flowering, you can either allow the plants to die back to their bulb until the following spring or you can plant them in the garden.

Propagation: The best way to propagate bulbs is from young offset bulbs produced by the parent. Pot them up into John Innes No. 1 potting compost, and they will flower a year or two later.

Pests and Diseases: Occasionally the first aphids of the year might attack your spring bulbs, or sometimes a passing slug or snail may make the most of an early spring feast!

CALCEOLARIA*

Calceolarias have curious 'inflated' balloon-like flowers that range from yellow to orange and red, and are often spotted. The plants are low growing and sport the flowers on relatively short stems.

General Care: Calceolarias love cool, light airy conditions and therefore prefer a well-ventilated greenhouse. They are not at all happy in hot, dry

Yellow-flowering calceolaria

conditions. To get the best from your plants, try to prevent them from drying out and, if anything, keep them moist most of the time. A temperature range of 10-15°C (50-60°F) is ideal.

Calceolarias are normally grown as annuals from seed, providing a fairly long season of colourful and unusual flowers before fading. If kept over winter, they need a minimum temperature of 7°C (45°F).

Propagation: Calceolarias are fairly easily raised from seed germinated in the early

spring. Sow in trays or half pots of seed compost and maintain at about 18°C (65°F). The seedlings should be pricked out when large enough to handle and potted up singly into potting compost using a minimum sized pot of 9 cm (3½ inches), a more suitable size being 13 cm (5 inches).

Pests and Diseases: Aphids are particularly fond of calceolarias and a close watch should always be kept for these pests. Whitefly can also be troublesome.

47

CAMPANULA*

The campanula most grown in the greenhouse is *Campanula isophylla*, commonly known as the 'bellflower'. It has green-grey heart-shaped leaves and is available with white or blue flowers. It makes a magnificent hanging basket plant.

General Care: *Campanula isophylla* is fairly adaptable and grows equally well in full light or slightly shaded situations. It does, however, prefer a relatively cool position and is not at all happy under hot, dry conditions. During the spring and summer, try to prevent the plant from drying out, but conversely take care not to overwater.

After flowering, trim the plant back at the end of the summer and keep it on the dry side in winter at a minimum temperature of 7°C (45°F). It

Carnations need a well-lit position

should be grown in 13 cm (5 inch) pots or hanging baskets of John Innes No. 3 potting compost. Campanula may also be grown outside during the warmer months of the year, although it is more likely to put on a good show of flowers under glass.

Propagation *Campanula isophylla* is relatively easily propagated from cuttings about 5-7.5 cm (2-3 inches) long, taken in April. Dip into hormone rooting powder and insert in a mixture of 2 parts of a loam-based seed compost to 1 part of fine sand. Insert three to five cuttings in a 9 cm (3½ inch) pot.

Pests and Diseases: Campanulas are sometimes troubled by aphids.

CARNATION*

Carnations and dianthus provide relatively easy-to-grow subjects for the greenhouse. The colour range varies from white to pink and red; and many newer varieties have striped or dark-edged petals. Some have a magnificent clove scent.

General Care: Dwarf varieties of dianthus can be grown in 13 cm (5 inch) pots of John Innes No. 2 potting compost. Carnations tend to grow taller and are happier grown in a growing bag. Depending on the size of the bag, plant them 10-15 cm (4-6 inches) apart, approximately 12 to a bag, and provide support with canes or mesh. Only the central bud of each shoot should be allowed to develop if large blooms are required.

Dianthus and carnations do

not like too much water, but they should not be allowed to dry out completely. Light is most important, for these plants like plenty of direct light and will grow leggy, producing less flowers, in the shade. Over winter keep them at about 4°C (40°F), trimming back as required to avoid unnecessary straggly growth at a time when space should not be wasted.

Propagation: Propagation can be achieved by cuttings taken during the spring and summer. Use side shoots, about 7.5-10 cm (3-4 inches) long. Dip into hormone rooting powder and root in seed compost and fine sand in a 2:1 ratio. Pot up the rooted cuttings in 7.5 cm (3 inch) pots.

Alternatively you can raise some varieties from seed by germinating seed in January at around 18°C (65°F) in a half pot of seed compost. Pot up when seedlings are large enough to handle.

Pests and Diseases: Red spider mites, aphids and thrips may sometimes attack.

CELOSIA*

Celosias, commonly called cockscomb, are annuals that flower through the summer, after which their life-cycle is completed and the plants die. The feathery flowers range in colour from yellow to red and are borne on plants about 20 cm (8 inches) tall. They provide a splash of colour in the greenhouse.

General Care: Celosias love lots of light and should be exposed to maximum sunlight, so do not hide them in any shady corners of your greenhouse. They also have a fair appetite for water and should not be allowed to dry out. The flowers last for quite a time before fading, after which the plants should be disposed of. Grow them in 9-13 cm (3½ -5 inch) pots of John Innes No. 1 potting compost.

Propagation: Celosias are easy to raise from seed in February. Sow seeds in a half pot filled with seed compost, lightly covering the seed, and keep at about 18°C (65°F). When germinated, the seedlings should be potted up singly in 9 cm (3½ inch) pots of potting compost and grown on.

Pests and Diseases: Celosia may be attacked by aphids.

Celosia (cockscomb)

Display of assorted chrysanthemums

CHRYSANTHEMUM*

Chrysanthemums come in an enormous variety of colours and forms: orange, pink, purple or red, and in tight pompoms or loose sprays. The small chrysanthemums grown by specialists as houseplants have been sprayed with growth-retardant chemicals, but the amateur will find that chrysanthemums need a fair amount of space and are perhaps happiest when grown in a growing bag in a greenhouse. They normally reach a height of 1.2-1.5 metres (4-5 ft).

General Care: In spring plant in growing bags, allowing about 12 plants per bag. The chrysanthemums will need plenty of light and a moderate temperature, although when established they will tolerate temperatures around 7°C (45°F). Keep the compost in the bags moist and do not allow them to dry out. The plants will require support in the form of canes or a mesh frame. Normally, they will flower as the days shorten in October and November, although they can flower at other times of the year with the correct treatment.

To make chrysanthemums flower out of season, cover them up with black polythene overnight a few hours before it is dark, and remove the cover several hours after sunrise. The black polythene should be placed *over* the plants and not *on them*, so you will need to construct a light frame. The procedure should be repeated every evening until the flower buds have formed. This treatment gives the plants an artificially short day and long night and thus encourages them to flower out of their natural season.

Propagation: Chrysanthemums are easily propagated in spring by taking cuttings about 7.5-10 cm (3-4 inches) long. Root them in 9 cm (3½ inch) pots of seed compost and allow to root well and grow on a little before planting up in a growing bag.

Pests and Diseases: Chrysanthemums are occasionally subject to attack by aphids, red spider mites, leaf miners, whitefly and thrips.

CINERARIA*

Although the correct name for this plant is *Senecio cruentus*, it is almost always listed as cineraria. A well-grown plant when the leaves are almost submerged beneath a mound of vivid daisy-like flowers in late winter and early spring, it is one of the most splendid sights in the greenhouse.

General care: The plants are best treated as biennials – sow them one year to flower the next, then discard them.

Cinerarias do not need much heat – 10°C (50°F) is ample, and it will not matter if the temperature drops a little below this. They do require shade from direct sun; a bright but shaded position, and a humid atmosphere, will produce good plants.

Propagation: Sow the seed in half pots from April to June. Cover with glass or polythene and keep moist and shaded until they germinate. When about three leaves have formed prick off into seed trays or small pots. Gradually move the plants on into 11 cm (4½ inch) and then into 15 cm (6 inch) pots. A peat-based or loam-based compost can be used. Feed the plants from autumn until they come into flower.

Pests and Diseases: If aphids do not try to make a meal of your cinerarias, you are lucky. Be vigilant, and spray with a suitable insecticide as soon as you notice them.

CYCLAMEN*

Cyclamen grow well in a greenhouse under the right conditions. Cyclamen, such as the silver-leaved strain with colourful foliage, and the diminutive mini-cyclamen are both available in a wide range of flower colours from white to pink, rose, salmon, red and lilac. They grow about 15-20 cm (6-8 inches) high.

General Care: Cyclamens like cool, light, airy conditions, so remember to ventilate the greenhouse well and do not allow the plants to become too hot. Keep them reasonably moist and avoid the compost in the pots drying out. They usually flower in the winter and continue to do so for several weeks.

After flowering, the leaves start to yellow. Stop watering and let the corms dry out. When the plants have rested for a few weeks, they may be started into growth again.

Do not allow the temperature to fall below 7°C (45°F), and aim to maintain a temper-

Red and white flowering cyclamens

ature of 13°C (55°F). When individual flowers or leaves die, remove them, otherwise they will rot and allow grey mould fungus (botrytis) to infect the plant.

Propagation: Cyclamen are propagated from seed. Sow the seeds in August or January at about 18°C (65°F) in a half pot of seed compost. When the seedlings are large enough to handle, pot up singly in 9 cm (3½ inch) pots of John Innes No. 1 potting compost. After a few months, they can be potted up into their final 13 cm (5 inches) pots, this time in John Innes No. 2 potting compost. When planting, take care to plant the corms proud

of the surface of the compost and do not bury them.

Pests and Diseases: Cyclamen are subject to attack by aphids, thrips and botrytis.

ECHINOPSIS*

The echinopsis is a popular cactus that grows to a height of 15 cm (6 inches). It is globe shaped and has prominent ribs. The flowers are truly magnificent and tend to dwarf the plant. Sometimes they are scented and the colour range varies from white to pink and yellow. Although the flowers last for only a few days, they are usually produced in sufficient numbers to give a good display.

General Care: Fortunately, echinopsis is very easy to keep and very tough. This makes it a superb cactus to grow in a cool greenhouse, provided it is frost-proof. During the winter, echinopsis should be kept cool and dry at a minimum temperature of about 7°C (45°F), although it may tolerate lower temperatures. During spring, as the light increases and it becomes warmer under glass, the cactus should be watered, allowing the compost to dry out in between waterings. Within a few weeks there will be a magnificent display of flowers.

Echinopsis should be grown in 10-15 cm (4-6 inch) pots of John Innes No. 2 potting compost, and given maximum light.

Propagation: Echinopsis are easily raised from seed, but you will have to be patient and wait a few years for them to become large enough to flower. Sow the seed in March in a half pot or seed tray in a mixture of seed compost and fine sand in a 4:1 ratio, sprinkling a little fine sand over the seed. Keep at about 20°C (68°F) until the seeds have germinated, then pot up singly when they are large enough to handle.

Pests and Diseases: Mealy bugs and root mealy bugs sometimes attack echinopsis.

EPIPHYLLUM**

The epiphyllum or orchid cactus is a magnificent cactus, producing some of the largest and most exotic flowers in the plant world. The flowers range in colour from white to yellow-orange, pink, lilac and red and are borne on green fleshy stems in spring. The blossoms measure from 5-15 cm (2-6 inches) across. The stems are flattened and have wavy edges, growing to a height of 90 cm (3 ft).

General Care: Epiphyllums are certainly worthy of a place in your greenhouse, especially as they need little care or attention. Through the spring and summer they should be grown in a slightly shaded situation, unlike other cacti which generally prefer full light. They should be allowed to dry out in between waterings, but generally prefer a little more water than many other cacti. In winter, keep the plants on the dry side at a temperature of about 10°C (50°F). A cool, dry winter followed by a warm and more moist spring and summer helps to initiate a good flush of flowers.

Propagation: Epiphyllums can be propagated from stem cuttings or from seed. The cuttings taken in early summer should be dipped into hormone rooting powder and then inserted into seed compost to root.

Seed can be germinated in April at about 20°C (68°F), sown in a mixture of seed compost and fine sand mixed at a ratio of 4:1. When large enough to handle, the seedlings should be pricked out and potted up in John Innes No. 2 potting compost. The plants should be potted on until they are in 15-20 cm (6-8 inch) pots.

Pests and Diseases: Mealy bugs, root mealy bugs, and sometimes aphids, may attack the plants.

Tall-growing fuchsia plants

FUCHSIA*

Fuchsias are extremly popular flowering plants that bloom for much of the summer both indoors and outside. The colours range from white, pink and red to a vivid magenta and deep violet. Plants can be tall-growing, bushy, or trailing. They vary in height from 15 cm (6 inches) to 60 cm (2 ft). Under glass, it is worth growing some of the less hardy and more choice varieties.

General Care: Fuchsias like a well-lit position in your greenhouse and should not be shaded at all. Try to ensure that they are kept relatively moist, and do not allow them to dry out. Pinching out the growing tips helps to maintain balanced, bushy growth.

Fuchsias will happily tolerate low temperatures over winter during their dormant period, although there are many varieties that prefer protection from frost. They must be kept dry until regrowth appears in spring. Pruning back in the autumn encourages better shaped plants for the following season.

Fuchsias should be grown in 15-20 cm (6-8 inch) pots of John Innes No. 3 potting compost.

Propagation: Fuchsias are extremely easy to propagate from cuttings of young shoots, about 7.5 cm (3 inches) long, taken in spring or summer. Dip them into hormone rooting powder before inserting into potting compost, preferably one cutting to a 9 cm (3½ inch) pot. Leave them to grow on, potting up as necessary.

Pests and Diseases: Fuchsias are prone to attack by aphids, whitefly and red spider mites.

GERANIUMS*

The plants commonly known as 'geraniums' but more correctly 'pelargoniums' – are very easy to grow. Like fuchsias, they make excellent flowering pot plants. There are many varieties suitable for growing in the greenhouse, and they fall into three main groups.

Zonal pelargoniums grow fairly large – up to 1.5 metres (5 ft) if allowed to, and hold their flower stems well clear of the plant.

Regal pelargoniums are about 40-50 cm (16-20 inches) high and bushy in habit.

Ivy-leaved pelargoniums are trailing in habit and suitable for hanging baskets.

General Care: Geraniums prefer an airy, well-lit position in

Pink and salmon coloured geraniums (pelargoniums)

the greenhouse and should not be kept too warm. Watering should be carried out with care, as overwatering can cause rapid death. The plants should be grown in 10-15 cm (4-6 inch) pots of John Innes No. 2 potting compost. During the summer, the plants may be placed outside, although they must receive protection from frosts in the winter. They are relatively happy with a winter temperature of about 7°C (45°F) provided that they are kept on the dry side. Trimming back the plants in the autumn will help them last the winter satisfactorily.

Propagation: Propagation is easy. Take cuttings about 7.5 cm (3 inches) long in late summer, dipping into hormone rooting powder and then into a 9 cm (3½ inch) pot of seed compost.

Some varieties can be grown from seed germinated in February in seed compost at a temperature of about 18-20°C (65-68°F), potting up when large enough. Choose suitable F_1 hybrids of the Zonal type if you want them to flower well in the first year.

Pests and Diseases: Certain varieties may be troubled by whitefly, botrytis (grey mould) and a rust fungus.

HIBISCUS**

The Chinese rose, *Hibiscus rosa-sinensis*, is a truly exotic plant growing to a height of 1.8 metres (6 ft) with superb large flowers that measure about 10 cm (4 inches) across. The colours vary from pink to salmon and red. Although short-lived, usually only a day or two, these flowers are produced in profusion. The foliage is dark green with the exception of the variegated variety which has green and white foliage. The red flowers of this variety are far less numerous, but last longer.

General Care: Hibiscus like a lot of light and thrive in the warm, well-lit conditions of a greenhouse. They are, however, sensitive to temperature fluctuations which can cause rapid flower bud drop. Keep them relatively warm in summer at around 18°C (65°F), and moist. Occasional trimming of the plants will help to maintain well-shaped plants, followed by hard pruning in the

early part of winter when hibiscus should be kept on the dry side and at a temperature of about 10-13°C (50-55°F). They should be grown in 20-30 cm (8-12 inch) pots of John Innes No. 2 potting compost or a soil-less compost.

Propagation: Hibiscus can be propagated, but they require a lot of care. Take tip cuttings, 7.5-10 cm (3-4 inches) long, in summer. Dip into hormone rooting powder and then insert into 9 cm (3½ inch) pots of seed compost. To reduce water loss from the cuttings, either mist with tepid water or cover with polythene until rooted. When fully established and grown on reasonably well, pot up into 13 cm (5 inch) pots of potting compost.

Pests and Diseases: Aphids can be a nuisance; red spider mites may also be a problem.

HYDRANGEA*

Although hydrangeas are normally grown outside, they also make good pot plants if grown carefully. The wide range of colourful and showy flowers make hydrangeas one of the most attractive flowering plants from early spring to late summer.

Grow in a pot as a small specimen with one large bloom, or in a tub as a branching shrub up to 1.2 metres (4 ft) high.

General Care: Hydrangeas like lots of light and, as their name suggests, they also like lots of water. Dehydration of the compost in the tightly massed fibrous rootball can cause severe damage, and even kill the plants. They should be grown in 15-20 cm (6-8 inch) pots of John Innes

No. 2 or No. 3 potting compost. If possible, keep in a cool part of the greenhouse otherwise they may become too leggy and soft. Blue-flowering varieties should be grown in lime-free compost. Watering with aluminium sulphate or alum helps to keep the blooms blue, and prevents them from turning pink or purple, which they do if the soil is alkaline. (Do not try to 'blue' pink or white varieties.)

The occasional application of Sequestrene will also help to combat effects of iron deficiency, which shows as a yellowing of the leaves between the veins. After flowering and at the end of the summer, hydrangeas should be pruned back fairly hard to overwinter satisfactorily, and kept just moist in a cool but frost-free position until the leaves begin to show in January or February. They can then be brought into a warmer position and watered freely.

Propagation: Hydrangeas are easily propagated from non-flowering shoots in July. Dip the cuttings into hormone rooting powder and then into a mixture of equal parts seed and potting compost. Dehydration of the cuttings may be reduced by misting them with tepid water or by covering with polythene. Pot the rooted cuttings up one to a 9

Blue-flowering hydrangeas

cm (3½ inch) pot of John Innes No. 2 potting compost and overwinter in a cool place.

Pests and Diseases: Hydrangeas may be attacked by aphids, red spider mites, mildew and eelworm. The latter deforms the leaves and reduces vigour. Plants affected by this pest are best destroyed, for control is difficult.

IMPATIENS*

The impatiens grown as a pot plant is the popular 'busy Lizzie'. It is very easy to grow and provides a long-lasting display of flowers throughout spring and summer. The foliage varies in colour from clear green to variegated and even purple; the flowers range from white to pink and red. Some of the plants can grow to a height of almost 60 cm (2 ft), but most modern varieties are much more compact than this.

General Care: Impatiens will grow well in partial shade but appreciate good light provided that it is not too strong through unshaded glass. They also require copious amounts of water; if allowed to dry out they will dehydrate and die. During spring and summer occasional pinching or trimming will encourage the plants to maintain a better shape, otherwise they tend to become leggy.

In late autumn, trim the plants back by as much as half to two-thirds and keep them on the dry side, then they will tolerate temperatures down to 7°C (45°F). Water more freely again when the warmer temperature and increased light of spring is conducive to renewed growth.

Grow in 13 cm (5 inch) pots of soil-less compost or John Innes No. 1 potting compost.

Propagation: Impatiens are easy to propagate. You can either take 7.5-10 cm (3-4 inch) long shoots and root them in a tumbler of water, or to do it more correctly, dip the cutting into hormone rooting powder and insert into a pot of seed compost. Whichever procedure you adopt, pot up the rooted cuttings into 7.5 cm (3 inch) pots.

Pests and Diseases: Impatiens are prone to attack by aphids, whitefly, red spider mites and mildew.

MAMMILLARIA*

Of all the cacti grown, mammillaria must be the most popular. It is fairly typical of what most people imagine a cactus to be with tubercles and spines arranged in spirals around the plant. The plants grow from 5-20 cm (2-8 inches) high depending on species. It is fairly free-flowering in summer with the flowers ranging from white to pink, rose-pink, lilac-pink and yellow. The arrangement of the flowers is normally in a ring around the top of the plant.

General Care: Like most cacti, mammillaria likes lots of light all through the year, with a reasonable amount of water throughout the spring and summer. Allow the plant to dry out in between waterings. During the winter, it should be kept on the dry side and at a

Pink and red impatiens (busy Lizzies)

temperature of about 10°C (50°F). This treatment is important in encouraging the plant to flower the following year. Most mammillarias, with the right treatment, will flower every year.

Propagation: Mammillaria may either be propagated from offsets teased away from the mother plant in summer and potted up separately in a mixture of 4 parts seed compost to 1 part fine sand, or from seed sown in spring in the same mixture and lightly covered with fine sand. A temperature of around 20°C (68°F) is required until the seeds have germinated. The seedlings should be left in the container until large enough to handle, and then potted up singly in 7.5 cm (3 inch) pots of gritty compost such as 2 parts John Innes No. 2 potting compost to 1 part coarse sand or grit. Pot on to larger pots in spring.

Pests and Diseases: The mammillaria cactus is subject to attack from mealy bugs and root mealy bugs.

POLYANTHUS*

With so much happening in your greenhouse during the spring and summer it is useful to know that polyanthus can make a good bridge between the winter and early spring. The leaves are only slightly larger than those of a wild primrose, but the flowers are grown on strong stems held clear of the foliage and come in vivid colours of white, yellow, pink, red or blue. They flower from Christmas to Easter.

General Care: Polyanthus are easy to grow and also frost-hardy. Growing the plants

Blue polyanthus – in flower from Christmas to Easter

under glass helps them to flower earlier. Polyanthus should not be cossetted and they prefer cool, well-lit conditions. They should be kept moist at all times, but without waterlogging the compost. Grow in 10-13 cm (4-5 inch) pots of John Innes No. 2 potting compost. Once flower stems are seen, feed weekly with liquid fertilizer.

When flowering is over, and certainly by the time you need the space in the greenhouse, from March or April onwards, you can remove the plants and plant them in the garden if you wish, to flower there next spring.

Propagation: Polyanthus may be propagated by division after flowering, or from seed. Seed should be sown in spring in a half pot or tray filled with seed compost and lightly covered. Keep moist and at a temperature of about 18°C (65°F) until germinated. When large enough to handle, prick out the seedlings and pot up separately in 9 cm (3½ inch) pots of potting compost. Pot into their final size pots by autumn.

Pests and Diseases: Polyanthus may be attacked by aphids and botrytis (grey mould) which causes black or brown leaf spots.

57

Yellow-flowering rebutias

REBUTIA*

Rebutia is quite an amazing cactus that produces a mass of flowers around the base of the plant, almost dwarfing it. Although this tiny globe-shaped cactus grows only about 5 cm (2 inches) in diameter, the mass of white, yellow, orange or red flowers that it produces virtually every year makes it a must for the greenhouse collection.

General Care: The rebutia is one of the easiest cacti to keep, and requires no special treatment. Like most cacti, it prefers a well-lit situation and to be allowed to dry out in between waterings during the spring and summer. In the winter, it should be kept almost completely dry and at a temperature around 10°C (50°F) as this will help to encourage it to flower the following year. It prefers a rich compost with added grit or sand, and it is usual to grow several plants in a 15 cm (6 inch) half pot or shallow pan. The flowers appear in early summer and are produced in profusion. In the evening the trumpet-like flowers close up, only to re-open the next morning for several days until they finally die.

Propagation: Rebutias freely set seed and this can be easily germinated when sown in a half pot or tray containing a mixture of 4 parts seed compost to 1 part fine sand. The seed should be lightly covered with fine sand and kept reasonably moist at a temperature of around 20°C (68°F) until it has germinated. Pot up the seedlings when large enough to handle.

Pests and Diseases: Mealy bugs, root mealy bugs and aphids may attack rebutias.

RHIPSALIDOPSIS*

Not all cacti are 'spiky barrels'; *Rhipsalidopsis gaertneri*, the Easter cactus, grows to 45 cm (18 inches), has flattish green pads and a few bristles at the end of the pads. It is naturally a tree-living cactus and requires slightly different treatment from its relations. The beauty of the Easter cactus lies not in its strange foliage and unusual appearance but in the magnificent display of flowers that the plant produces each year. The blossoms are superb, 5-6 cm (2-2½ inch) long red trumpets that literally cover the plant with a superb blaze of colour. It flowers, as you might expect, in March and April.

General Care: In order to encourage the plant to flower well, it should be kept on the dry side in winter, watering only to avoid dehydration. A temperature of around 10-13°C (50-55°F) is suitable. In spring, the warmer condition will mean that the plant requires more water, although it should not be kept constantly moist. Keeping the greenhouse damped down with water will provide the humid conditions it prefers. Feed weekly with dilute liquid fertilizer while flowering.

Unlike many other cacti, rhipsalidopsis does not like too much direct sunlight and should therefore be placed in a position where it has some light shade. As it lives perched on branches of trees in its natural habitat, it does not need an ordinary compost, but is best in a mixture of leafmould and sandy grit. Grow it in 13 cm (5 inch) pots.

After flowering, the plant will produce new growth in the form of little leaf pads that grow past the withering and rapidly dropping dead flowers. It can be stood outside in the summer in a shady place.

Propagation: The Easter cactus can be propagated from mature leaf pads, gently pulled from the plant. Dip these into hormone rooting powder and then insert two or three pads to a 9 cm (3½ inch) pot of seed compost. Once rooted, leave to grow on in the same pot.

Pests and Diseases: Easter cacti may be attacked by mealy bugs and root mealy bugs.

SAINTPAULIA**

Saintpaulias, the popular African violets, form a close rosette of fleshy, hairy leaves from which pretty flowers arise in a wide range of colours – usually purple/blue, but also white, pink, wine-red, light blue, and dark blue. There are even bi-coloured and frilled forms.

General Care: African violets prefer a temperature of about 20°C (68°F), shaded from direct sunlight. You can even place them beneath the staging. Humidity is important but avoid splashing water on the leaves, which are easily marked. Water the plants from below, placing the pot in a saucer and allow it to soak up what it requires within about 20 minutes before pouring away the surplus.

A stubborn African violet can be coaxed into flower by keeping the plant on the dry side for six to eight weeks, watering only if it looks like drying out and dying. Then gradually increase the water, and feed every two weeks with tomato fertilizer at about quarter strength.

Propagation: Take leaf cuttings. Select a mature leaf, and cut it off cleanly at the base of the leaf stalk close to the centre of the plant. Cut back the leaf stalk to about 3-4 cm (1½ inches) and lightly dip into hormone rooting powder. Gently insert the stalk into a 5 cm (2 inch) pot of seed compost, leaving a small space between the base of the leaf and the compost surface. Cover the leaf with polythene. The cuttings should root in about six to eight weeks, but it may be as long again before plantlets emerge. Pot on into 9 cm (3½ inch) pots.

Pests and Diseases: Aphids and mildew can be problems during spring and summer; botrytis (grey mould) is a risk at any time.

Pink saintpaulias (African violets)

Solanum capsicastrum (winter cherry)

SELENICEREUS*

The selenicereus is a magnificent cactus to grow in your greenhouse. The flowers are superb, varying in colour from white to yellow, scarlet or mauve and measure up to 20 cm (8 inches) across, often with a fantastic scent. *Selenicereus grandiflorus*, which grows about 1.8 metres (6 ft) tall, is called the 'queen of the night' as it flowers at night.

General Care: To grow this selenicereus successfully, provide the plant with support and a well-lit position. During the winter, keep it on the dry side and at a temperature of around 13°C (55°F), watering only to prevent dehydration. Water more frequently during the spring and summer, allowing the plant to get on the dry side before re-watering.

Provide support in the form of canes or a trellis, for the growth habit can be rather straggly. It can also be grown against the wall of the greenhouse. Finally, you will need a torch! The splendid flowers of the selenicereus open at night and you will only see them at their best if you go to look at them then. It is well worth the trouble!

Propagation: Selenicereus may be propagated from cuttings in a similar way to rhipsalidopsis, or from seed germinated at about 20°C (68°F) in a mixture of 4 parts seed compost to 1 part fine sand. Prick out and pot up singly when large enough to handle.

Pests and Diseases: Mealy bugs and root mealy bugs sometimes attack this plant.

SOLANUM*

Solanum capsicastrum or winter cherry is a fairly compact plant from the same family as the tomato. It bears small white flowers and has rich green leaves. Once pollinated the plant produces orange, cherry-like fruits that look attractive and decorative. The fruits are inedible and indeed poisonous. It grows to a height of up to 45 cm (18 inches).

General Care: The winter cherry is very easy to grow, provided it is given plenty of light and is not allowed to dry out, particularly during the critical time of flowering and the period of fruit setting. It is hardy enough to be grown outside for the summer but should be given protection under glass from September onwards. By early autumn the fruit will appear and will gradually colour to provide a magnificent display over the Christmas period. Spraying the plant with a mist of tepid water during the flowering period will help to 'set' the flowers and will encourage a better show of fruit. Feed every two weeks with dilute liquid fertilizer from June until the fruits ripen.

Over the winter period, this solanum is happy with a minimum temperature of around 10°C (50°F), which makes it an easy and colourful plant to grow in the greenhouse at a time when little else is happening. It is grown in 13 cm (5 inch) pots of John Innes No. 2 potting compost and is usually treated as an annual.

Propagation: The winter cherry is easily propagated from seed germinated in seed compost at about 18-20°C (65-68°F) in the spring. When large enough to handle, prick out and pot up the seedlings separately in potting compost. Pinch out the growing tips to produce bushy plants.

Pests and Diseases: Solanums are occasionally attacked by aphids and are particularly prone to white fly.

STREPTOCARPUS*

Streptocarpus or Cape primroses are rather unusual flowering plants of low habit, growing to 20-30 cm (8-12 inches) in height. They produce pink, red, purple or lilac primrose-like, but tubular, flowers. The longish leaves radiate in opposite directions generally in pairs.

General Care: Streptocarpus should be kept at about 10°C (50°F) over winter, and just moist. From March onwards they prefer a slightly higher temperature but should not be exposed to full light all the time because they appreciate a certain amount of light shade.

Water freely in summer. The plants will then flower from May right through until October. Grow in 13-20 cm (5-8 inch) pots of John Innes No. 2 potting compost or a soil-less compost.

Propagation: Streptocarpus can either be propagated from seed or from leaf cuttings. Seed should be sown at about 21°F (70°F) in seed compost in half pots or seed trays in spring, potting the seedlings up singly in 13 cm (5 inch) pots of potting compost.

Leaf cuttings are taken in a most unusual way. Cut off a semi-mature leaf (not one too old or too young). Cut the leaf in half down the central main vein and then cut each half into pieces about 2.5 cm (1 inch) wide. Dip the area of the main vein into hormone rooting powder and then lightly insert into seed compost in seed trays or half pots containing a mixture of peat and sand. Cover with polythene or apply a mist of tepid water to reduce water loss. When rooted, pot up singly in 9 cm (3½ inch) pots of potting compost.

Pests and Diseases: Aphids can be a problem.

Streptocarpus (Cape primroses) and Saintpaulia

FRUIT AND VEGETABLES

It is hardly surprising that the most popular things grown in a greenhouse are edible.

Sadly, many people tend to grow only tomatoes or – if they are a little more adventurous – cucumbers or peppers. However, with very little special care you can grow all sorts of exciting fruits and vegetables, such as apricots, courgettes, grapes, melons and even peaches.

To achieve good results it is not necessary to heat the greenhouse to an expensive extent. In fact, if grown in their natural season, the majority of fruit and vegetables manage without any artificial heat at all. Lettuce, rhubarb or strawberries can be grown with nothing more than sufficient heat to keep out the frost. For early or out of season crops, the greenhouse must be heated to the required temperature.

Effective use of space is essential when growing food crops under glass, to obtain a maximum yield. You may find that even with the best planning you wish that you had arranged things differently. Growing bags provide some flexibility because they can be moved relatively easily, unless of course the crops in them have become too tall.

Pots and troughs are also useful and, in the same way as growing bags, they isolate food crops from each other, reducing the likelihood of soil-borne diseases spreading. This can be a major problem with food crops grown under glass and planted in the border soil. Some plants will grow quite happily in border soil, but it is particularly important in the case of tomatoes to sterilize the soil in between crops, or avoid the problem altogether by using pots or growing bags.

APRICOTS*

Apricots are well worth growing in a greenhouse whether free standing or lean-to, provided you can give the plants enough room. Growing apricots under glass not only helps to ripen the fruit which would otherwise be more difficult and stubborn to ripen outside but also has another major benefit in avoiding frost damage to the flowers which bloom in February, earlier than most fruit trees.

General Care: Although apricots may be grown in pots for the first few years, they have such active root growth and so large an appetite, that they quickly out-grow their pots and are better in the border soil of the greenhouse. To save space, it is a good idea to buy fan-trained plants to grow against the lean-to wall or side of the greenhouse. Start the plants off in 25 cm (10 inch) pots of John Innes No. 2 potting compost and then move into larger tubs or into the border soil. Keep the plants well watered through the spring and summer and feed occasionally with tomato fertilizer.

It is not really necessary to prune in the first year but in the second year growth can be cut back by one third to a half to encourage compact growth and fruiting. Fruit set can be increased by hand pollinating the apricot flowers with a small artist's paint-brush, brushing the pollen of one flower onto the centre of another. Fortunately, it is quite sufficient to have only one plant as apricots are self-fertile. To produce better fruits, it is worthwhile thinning out the fruitlets to about 20 cm (8 inches) apart in June. The fruits can be harvested in

Ripe apricots – ready for harvesting

August when they are fully ripened and easy to remove.

Over winter, the plant should be kept cool, down to about 2°C (35°F), and a little on the dry side.

Propagation: Apricots can be propagated from apricot stones germinated at about 20°C (68°F) in 9 cm (3½ inch) pots of seed compost, buried about 5 cm (2 inches) deep. Leave the plants to grow on and pot up into larger pots when they are big enough to be transplanted.

Pests and Diseases: Apricots are subject to infection from peach leaf curl and leaf spot. You will need to spray with a copper compound to control peach leaf curl, following the manufacturer's instructions.

fruits should be harvested when large enough – about 10 cm (4 inches) in length and of a good colour. It is advisable to cut the fruit from the plant with a sharp knife rather than simply pulling it off.

Propagation: Germinate the seed in February at about 20-21°C (68-70°F) in either a seed tray or half pot of seed compost. Prick out and pot up the seedlings singly in 9 cm (3½ inch) pots of potting compost and grow on. Then, when about 15-20 cm (6-8 inches) tall, plant the aubergines in growing bags or pots of John Innes No. 2 or No. 3 potting compost.

Pests and Diseases: Aubergines are subject to attack from whitefly, red spider mites and occasionally botrytis (grey mould). The latter is a problem often caused by poor and damp growing conditions.

COURGETTES**

Courgettes grow particularly well in a greenhouse. Actually, courgettes are small marrows, or rather marrows that are picked earlier than they would be in the case of the more 'normal' sized vegetable. Varieties such as F_1 'Zucchini' and F_1 'Golden Zucchini' are good types to grow. They have a sprawling habit and they therefore take up quite a lot of room. However, if you like courgettes, then you probably will not mind the space they take up.

General Care: Plant them in growing bags, allowing about two plants to a bag. Take particular care not to allow the plants to dry out and to keep them well watered. Feeding should be started as soon as

AUBERGINES**

Aubergines are rather extraordinary plants, producing interesting fruits that are pear-shaped in appearance. The plants do not grow very tall but they do take up a fair amount of room. They can, however, be grown in pots or growing bags.

General Care: Grow the plants in either 20 cm (8 inch) pots, one to a pot, or growing bags, three to a growing bag. The plants like light and warmth. Although aubergines can be grown outside, they will grow far better under glass, producing more vigorous growth and more fruit of better quality.

The purple flowers should pollinate easily and fruit set should not be a problem. However, occasional misting with tepid water will help to increase the set if a problem is experienced. When the plant is large enough and the first fruit sets, start feeding once a week using a tomato fertilizer, applied at normal strength. As the plants grow, they will need support either in the form of canes if the plants are in pots, or a support frame if grown in growing bags. The

63

you have picked the first fruits, using a tomato fertilizer applied at the standard rate. The young marrows or courgettes are best harvested when they are up to 15 cm (6 inches) long. Harvesting the small fruits encourages the production of further fruits. If fruit set is found to be a problem, it may be encouraged with a small artist's paintbrush. Lightly tickle the flowers with the brush to transfer pollen from male to female flowers in order to pollinate them.

Propagation: Courgettes are best propagated by sowing seed in peat pots as this helps to avoid root disturbance when planting up later. In May sow one seed to each 9 cm (3½ inch) pot of seed compost, placing the seed on its edge in the moist compost without covering it. Keep the seed at about 21°C (70°F) to germinate and grow on in the individual pots until about 15 cm (6 inches) tall. Then transfer to the growing bags and grow on.

Pests and Diseases: Courgettes are subject to infestation of whitefly and red spider mites. They can also be infected with mildew.

CUCUMBERS**

Although cucumbers are a bit fiddly to grow, and can take up a fair amount of room in your greenhouse, they are worth experimenting with. Cucumbers grown under glass will produce fruits just like the ones that you can buy from the greengrocer rather than the ridge cucumbers with their characteristic rough skins that you would normally grow outside in the garden.

General Care: Cucumbers are rather susceptible to root rot problems which often occur when they are overwatered. To avoid this situation, it may help if you grow the plants in growing bags which have slits cut in the bottom edge of the sides to aid drainage. Plant two or three cucumber plants to a bag and provide support in the form of a growing bag support frame, canes, strings or wires. Strings or wires are probably the easiest method of providing support and work reasonably well. Anchor the string to the bag by tying it around the bag near each plant; then tie this to the greenhouse roof at a suitable anchorage point.

The plants should be planted during May to avoid frosts if your greenhouse is unheated, and when temperatures are about 15°C (60°F). Cucumbers prefer light shade and a humid environment. Keep the compost moist and start feeding with a tomato fertilizer as soon as the first fruits have been picked. Apart from training the plants around wires or whatever support you have used, you will need to work on the crops by removing any side shoots. Do not be too impatient for fruit; you will get better results by removing any flowers or fruit on the first 40-45 cm (16-18 inches) of stem and allowing ones above to grow normally.

All-female varieties are the best to grow as these will save you the trouble of pinching off the male flowers to prevent them from fertilizing the female flowers and spoiling the fruit. If fertilization takes place the fruit is bitter to taste.

Varieties such as 'Fertila', 'Monique' and 'Amstic' – all F_1 hybrids – are useful varieties that produce no male flowers. 'Amstic' is the most tolerant of lower temperatures.

Once the plants have grown to the greenhouse roof it is a good idea to let two to four side shoots trail down. This will help to increase the crop potential.

Propagation: Germinate the seed in February or March, one seed to a 9 cm (3½ inch) pot of seed compost. The use of a peat pot that can be planted directly avoids root disturbance. Keep the seed at about 21°C (70°F) to germinate, then grow on in the pot until the plants are about 15 cm (6 inches) high, when they can be transplanted.

Pests and Diseases: Cucumbers are prone to red spider mite, whitefly and mildew.

LEFT: Indoor cucumbers have a superior flavour

GRAPES*

If you can afford the time and space you might like to grow grapes in your greenhouse. Growing them under glass gives you the advantage of a more reliable crop than when grown outside, with larger berries and less susceptibility of frost damage to the flowers and young growth. It can be a delight to grow your own grapes, so they are probably worth the effort.

General Care: Grapes like a well-lit situation, and they should be planted in the greenhouse border soil and not in a tub or container. To save space, it may be worthwhile training them along the side of the greenhouse. Wires stretched along the length of the greenhouse and arched on sturdy posts placed at either end should provide a good support structure. In summer, when the plants bear fruit, maintain a temperature of 18°C (64°F). Keep the atmosphere humid at first, gradually increasing ventilation as the fruit nears maturity. Feeding with tomato fertilizer is useful but do not keep the grapes too well watered. During the winter it is advisable to let the vines be exposed to relatively low temperatures down to around 0°C (32°F) to provide the dormant season that they need.

Pruning grapes is an art in itself. In the autumn choose one main stem to grow on the framework and cut back all side shoots to about half their length. In subsequent years train side shoots and the main

Grapes are best supported by horizontal wires

shoot to the shape you want, but cut back all other shoots to two buds of new wood. These buds produce the flowers the following year. When the flowers appear in April and May, pollinate them with a small brush, brushing pollen from one blossom on to another. When the fruit has set, occasional thinning of the berries helps to increase the size of the remaining fruit, if you want larger grapes for dessert purposes.

Propagation: Although it is tempting to grow grapes from pips, you will achieve a better result from cuttings. When

65

Lettuce seedlings – ready for planting out

full-sized growing bag, which is quite a crop from a bag that has already produced a crop of tomatoes. Grow them on, avoiding excessively wet, damp or cold conditions which could cause the lettuces to rot off. Lettuces like a well-lit situation in the greenhouse and should not be grown in shade. A temperature of 10°C (50°F) is needed for growing most winter-maturing varieties, but requirements vary.

Propagation: Lettuces should be germinated either in half pots or seed trays of seed compost. Sow the seed thinly and lightly cover with compost. Keep moist, and provide a temperature of about 13-15°C (55-60°F) until germinated. Avoid temperatures above this, otherwise germination may be inhibited. When the seedlings are large enough to handle, about 5-7.5 cm (2-3 inches) tall, prick them out and plant out.

Pests and Diseases: Lettuces are subject to attack from aphids, slugs, mildew and botrytis (grey mould).

MELONS**

Melons are interesting and slightly more unusual plants for the greenhouse. They can be grown either in pots or growing bags. However, the choice of variety is fairly crucial to success. Some of the varieties may be disappointing in this climate, but one that is certainly worth trying is the 'Ogen' melon, a Canteloupe type that is very suited to cool greenhouse culture.

General Care: Either plant the

you prune back the grape vines in winter cut up the lengths into pieces about 25 cm (10 inches) long and insert them in the greenhouse border soil leaving the top of the shoot just above the surface of the soil. Use a cane or even a garden fork to make suitable sized holes for them. Then leave them to root and grow on, transplanting them when you wish, preferably about a year after insertion.

Pests and Diseases: Grapes are subject to attack from mildew.

LETTUCE*

Lettuce can be grown in a greenhouse at any time of the year and the quality is normally far better than when grown outside. Greenhouse lettuces are especially useful in winter, however, when shop prices are high and it is not possible to harvest an outdoor crop.

There are several types of lettuce: cabbage, crisphead,

cos and 'cut-and-come-again'. Success or failure depends very much on the choice of variety if you are growing out of season. You must select a variety that is suitable for the temperature you can maintain (heat is not essential), and sow it at the recommended time. A good seed catalogue will suggest suitable varieties.

General Care: Lettuces can either be grown directly in the greenhouse border soil or in growing bags. Using the previous season's growing bags for growing lettuce after a tomato crop is a good idea and makes best use of your resources. Varieties such as 'Kloek' for spring cutting, 'Plus' for cropping from mid-October to mid-April and 'Fortune' for summer cutting are all good varieties, but follow the earlier advice on selecting a variety.

You can plant up to 12 lettuces, in two rows of six, in a

Ogen melons are suited to cool greenhouse culture

melons in 25 cm (10 inch) pots of John Innes No. 3 potting compost or plant three to a growing bag. Keep relatively moist and start to feed with a tomato fertilizer when the plants are about 30 cm (1 ft) tall. Tie the plants to a support cane or framework. When the flowers open help the plants by tickling the flowers with a small artist's paint-brush, transferring pollen from male to female flowers. This will help pollinate them and encourage fruit set. As the fruits get larger tie them in nets to the framework to ripen, and ventilate well to prevent mildew. It is wise to settle for four melons to a plant, removing further fruits if they develop.

Propagation: Germinate the seeds individually in 9 cm (3½ inch) pots of seed compost, lightly inserting each seed on its edge into the surface but not covering it. To avoid root disturbance at transplanting, use peat pots, planting up when the plants have produced about four or five leaves.

Pests and Diseases: Melons may be attacked by whitefly or botrytis (grey mould).

MUSTARD AND CRESS*

Surely the easiest plants to grow must be mustard and cress. They provide a useful salad, garnish or sandwich filler at any time of the year.

General Care: The best way to grow mustard and cress is to sow the seed on to absorbent moist material such as blotting paper, paper tissue, cotton wool, or peat. Place any of these materials in a suitable container – a seed tray or plastic plant pot saucer are ideal. Sow the seed on to the surface of the material chosen and keep constantly moist. Be sure to check several times a day during warm, sunny conditions that the pots are not drying out, and within a few days the seeds will germinate.

White mustard will germinate quickly – within a few days – and can be eaten about a week after sowing, when it is about 2.5 cm (1 inch) high. Do not leave it any longer or it will become somewhat bitter. Cress takes a little longer. Although it germinates after about three to five days, it is usually not ready for harvest until two to three weeks after sowing. When mustard and cress are grown together harvest about 12 days after sowing.

Pests and Diseases: Fortunately, neither mustard nor cress should suffer from any pest or disease problem.

PEACHES*

Peaches should be grown in the same way as apricots. They need a fair amount of room, but growing them in a greenhouse is a good way to achieve a reasonable crop of fruits by ripening them more effectively.

General Care: Peaches may be grown in pots or tubs in the greenhouse, although they will grow better if planted directly in the border soil where the roots will not be so restricted and where the plants are not so likely to run short of nutrients. In the same way as for apricots, peaches can be trained in a fan shape against the greenhouse wall. To start the plants off, 25 cm (10 inch) pots of John Innes No. 2 potting compost can be used. The plants should be well watered throughout the spring and summer and fed with dilute tomato fertilizer.

After the first year, when pruning is not necessary, the second year's growth may be cut back to one third or half. In the same way as for apricots, fruit set may be increased by hand pollination of the flowers in March. This can be done easily by tickling the flowers with a small artist's paint-brush. Thin out the fruits in June if necessary and harvest the fruit in August or when it parts easily from the stalk. During winter allow the plants to be exposed to a temperature of about 2°C (35°F), and keep them on the dry side.

Peaches ripen more effectively in a greenhouse

Propagation In the same way as for apricots, peaches may be grown from stones planted about 5 cm (2 inches) deep in 9 cm (3½ inch) pots of seed compost, kept at about 20°C (68°F). Pot on when large enough to handle.

Pests and Diseases: Peaches may be attacked by peach leaf curl and leaf spot. Peach leaf curl is difficult to control once established, so it is worth spraying with a copper compound as a precaution (following manufacturer's advice).

PEPPERS*

Peppers are coming more into fashion as vegetables, although strictly they are fruits like tomatoes. These green or red fruits are produced freely throughout the summer and require little special care.

General Care: Peppers like warmth and light and do well in a greenhouse. Grow them either potted in John Innes No. 2 potting compost in 20-25 cm (8-10 inch) pots, or in growing bags, three to a bag. Peppers should be kept relatively moist and never allowed to dry out. It helps to spray the plants with tepid water during the flowering period. They should be fed with a tomato fertilizer when the plants have grown to about 15-20 cm (6-8 inches) tall, or as soon as the first fruits have set. When you have picked the first pepper, the plant will then 'break', producing side shoots from which future peppers will grow.

As far as the colour of peppers is concerned, the longer you leave them, the more time they are given to turn red.

Peppers are well worth space in the greenhouse

However, in order to get the maximum yield from your plants, it is better to pick them green and allow the plant to produce more rather than waiting and wasting crop potential. If necessary, provide support with a cane or framework.

Varieties worth growing are 'Canape' and 'Early Prolific' (both F_1 Hybrids), or for a yellow-coloured variety, 'Gold Star'. Peppers are not frost hardy and if your greenhouse is not heated, they should not be planted out until May.

Propagation: Sow in March in a seed tray or half pot of seed compost and lightly cover with compost. Keep at about 20°C (68°F) until germinated. When large enough to handle, prick out the seedlings singly into 9 cm (3½ inch) pots, using John Innes No. 1 potting compost. Grow on until about 15 cm (6 inches) tall before planting in growing bags or potting on.

Pests and Diseases: Aphids and whitefly can be problems.

PINEAPPLES*

Pineapples are only worth growing in a greenhouse if you are adventurous and curious to know how they grow. The chances of growing an edible pineapple are pretty remote, but the habit of growth is interesting with the small pineapple growing on a stalk from the centre of the rosette of spiky leaves.

General Care: Pineapples must have a well-lit position in the greenhouse. During the summer, they should be watered fairly regularly, being allowed to dry out a little between waterings. In winter they will tolerate temperatures down to 7°C (45°F) provided they are kept on the dry side. To encourage fruiting, cover the plants with polythene bags and place two or three ripe apples underneath each. After a week or so, remove the bags and the apples, and hope that the gas given off by the apples (ethylene) will have initiated the fruiting response. If they do not flower within a few months, repeat the treatment.

Propagation: The best way to propagate a pineapple is to cut the top off a fruit leaving 1 cm (½ inch) below the bottom rosette of leaves. Dust this with hormone rooting powder, then insert into a 13 cm (5 inch) pot containing a mixture of 3 parts seed compost to 1 part sand. Water infrequently until it starts to grow.

Pests and Diseases: Mealy bugs and root mealy bugs may attack pineapples.

RHUBARB*

Rhubarb is a useful plant, worth growing in the greenhouse in winter to provide a source of fresh material for culinary use. The effort necessary is minimal and you can grow, or rather force, it at a time when you probably have space free in the greenhouse.

General Care: During the winter, allow the rhubarb to be exposed to some fairly severe cold weather as this is important for successful forcing later on. If the winter is mild, dig up the rhubarb and expose to the frost for a few days. Then, during December, either place the crowns in a black polythene refuse sack and leave under the staging in the greenhouse, pulling the stalks once they have grown, or place in a box or other suitable container, planting in moist peat. Again, cover up the plant with black polythene until it has produced the sticks. A temperature of about 13-15°C (55-60°F) is suitable for forcing. After forcing, the clumps or roots of

Rhubarb can be grown or 'forced' under the staging

rhubarb will have been exhausted and should be disposed of.

Propagation: Rhubarb clumps are easily propagated. Simply use a spade and chop or lever the clump apart. Then plant or force as required. The best time to do this is during the winter.

Pests and Diseases: Luckily, rhubarb grown in the greenhouse is usually trouble-free.

STRAWBERRIES*

Both conventional strawberries such as 'Cambridge Favourite' and alpine varieties such as 'Alexandria' can be grown successfully in a greenhouse where they will produce an earlier crop than they would outdoors.

General Care: Strawberries do tend to take up a fair amount of space, especially if they are planted in the normal way flat on the ground. The best way to grow them, therefore, is either in a growing bag laid flat, planting two rows of five down the length, or alternatively with the bag on its end and slits, about 7.5-10 cm (3-4 inches) long, cut opposite

each other in pairs, to make a kind of strawberry 'barrel'.

Plant the strawberry plants in September and leave outside until January, when they can be brought under glass. Strawberries will flower in April. To encourage good fruiting, you can help pollinate the flowers by tickling with a small artist's paint-brush. With few insects around, this action in the early spring will help to ensure a better crop. Water as soon as the plants start to grow and keep moist while fruiting. Feed after fruiting with a tomato fertilizer. When the plants have fruited, the growing bag or pots, if you chose to use them, should then be placed outside.

Propagation: Strawberries can be propagated from the numerous runners produced in summer and potted up singly in 9 cm (3½ inch) pots of potting compost.

Alpine varieties can be raised from seed germinated at about 15-18°C (60-65°F). Prick out and pot up singly when seedlings are large enough to handle.

Pests and Diseases: Strawberries are subject to attack from aphids. These pests are a particular nuisance, because they also spread strawberry virus disease.

TOMATOES*

Of all the crops grown under glass, tomatoes are still by far the most popular. They are relatively easy to grow and, apart from the conventional types that take up quite a large amount of room, you can now grow smaller varieties that thrive well on the staging in pots.

General Care: Although tomatoes can be grown in border soil, they will grow far better with much less risk of any disease or infection by being planted three to a growing bag. Plant them up when frosts have finished if your greenhouse is unheated, when your plants are about 15 cm (6 inches) tall.

Keep the plants well watered in the bag and start feeding with a tomato fertilizer as soon as the first truss of tomatoes has set and the second truss is well on the way in terms of development. Pollination and fruit set might be a problem during the early spring and this can be helped either by spraying the flowers lightly with water or by gently shaking the plant to transfer pollen.

If you grow a normal variety, such as 'Moneymaker' or 'Eurocross A' which require support, you will need to pinch or rub out the side shoots, to encourage the plant to grow straight up. Support in the form of growing bag frames or strings tied around the bags and trained to the

Tomatoes – the most popular greenhouse crop

greenhouse roof will be important in taking the weight of the plants as they grow. Bush varieties such as 'Minibel' will only grow about 30 cm (12 inches) high and will not need to have their side shoots removed. They also grow well in 20-25 cm (8-10 inch) pots of John Innes No. 2 potting compost. The fruits are obviously smaller but taste very good.

Tomatoes need a temperature of about 15-18°C (60-65°F) when at the seedling stage but later they will tolerate a temperature down to about 10°F (50°F). Keep the plant well watered all the time they are fruiting as drying out can cause a disorder called 'blossom end rot', which causes the ends of the fruit to blacken and shrivel.

In the autumn, when the plants die, any green fruits can be encouraged to ripen by laying them in a warm place.

Propagation: Germinate the seed in the middle of March (or earlier if you heat your greenhouse) in seed trays or dwarf pots of seed compost covering the seed lightly. Keep at about 18-20°C (65-68°F) until germinated, then prick out and pot up singly when large enough to handle into 9 cm (3½ inch) pots of potting compost. Grow the plants on until 15 cm (6 inches) tall when they can be potted on or planted out.

Pests and Diseases: Tomatoes are subject to attack from whitefly, wilt diseases (particularly if planted direct into border soil) and botrytis (grey mould). Plants suffering from wilt are best destroyed and the soil or compost should not be used for tomatoes again.

CLIMBING PLANTS

Climbing plants are most useful in a greenhouse to provide natural, dappled shade and to fill the roof space.

It is, of course, essential to take into account the extent to which sunlight reaching the other plants is likely to be reduced by climbing plants. As a general rule foliage plants prefer heavier shade unlike flowering plants which require lighter shade. The passiflora or passion flower is most suiable if you want to create a dappled green, fairly heavy shade. At the other extreme, hoya and stephanotis – despite their fleshier leaves – are less densely foliaged and can be grown in parts of the greenhouse where more light is required.

Climbing plants are ideal for growing in association with a foliage plant collection. Both types will require some heat over the winter period if you are growing a more exotic collection, but with hardier species you can avoid expensive heating costs.

Keep the plants in containers so that they can easily be moved to other sites in the greenhouse. As far as support for the plants is concerned, you can use canes or thin wooden stakes in the early stages. Thin metal wires or horticultural twine are ideal for providing support from the bottom to the top of the greenhouse or along the roof to train the growth in a horizontal plane.

ABUTILON**

Strictly speaking, the abutilon or 'flowering maple' is not really a climber. However, its habit of growth is such that it makes an excellent background plant that grows up to 2 metres (6 ft) tall provided it is given some form of support. The hanging, bell-like flowers of the plant range from yellow to red in colour and are produced from May to October. Depending on the variety, abutilons have either green or variegated foliage.

General Care: Abutilons do not like hot dry conditions but otherwise they are reasonably easy to grow. Excessive amounts of sunlight may scorch the leaves, so some light shade should be given. The plants like to be kept reasonably moist during the growing season from April to late September. During the autumn and winter they require much less water, and should be kept on the dry side.

Abutilons will tolerate temperatures down to 10°C (50°F). Grow either in the greenhouse border or in 15-20 cm (6-8 inch) pots of John Innes No. 2 potting compost. Feed every two weeks from May to September with dilute tomato fertilizer.

Propagation: Abutilons can be germinated from seed. Sow in a half pot of seed compost in spring and maintain at a temperature of about 20°C (68°F) until germinated. Prick out and pot on singly into 9 cm (3½ inch) pots of John Innes No. 1 potting compost when large enough to handle.

Alternatively, propagate from cuttings, about 7.5 cm (3 inches) long, taken in summer and dipped into hormone rooting powder before inserting in 9 cm (3½ inch) pots of seed compost.

Pests and Diseases: Abutilon is subject to attack from aphids, red spider mites, root mealy bugs and scale insects.

BOUGAINVILLEA**

Bougainvilleas are quite extraordinary climbing plants that produce magnificent 'flowers'. The 'flowers' are in fact highly coloured bracts, ranging in colour from pink to orange red and even yellow. The small white true flowers are found in the centres of the bracts. The plants produce an abundance of bright bracts throughout the summer, for about three months. The plants grow to about 2.5 metres (10 ft) tall in pots or about 9 metres (30 ft) if grown in a greenhouse border, and provide a really superb addition to your collection, provided you have space.

General Care: Bougainvilleas are relatively easy to grow, enjoying a position in full light. During spring and summer, the plants must not be allowed to dry out or they may die. Occasional spraying with tepid water during warm dry conditions is beneficial.

During the winter, however, the plants should be kept on the dry side and watered much less frequently. They will then tolerate a temperature down to around 10°C (50°F). Following the winter, a light pruning back of shoots by about one quarter to one third will encourage compact, well-shaped growth from the spring onwards, but the plants will still require support either with a trellis, canes or strings. They should be grown in 15-20 cm (6-8 inch) pots of John Innes No. 3 potting compost.

Propagation: Bougainvilleas can be propagated by taking 7.5-10 cm (3-4 inches) long cuttings in summer, dipping into hormone rooting powder and then inserting into 5 cm (2 inch) pots of seed compost or a mixture of 4 parts seed compost to 1 part sand. Keep at about 24°C (70°F).

Pests and Diseases: Aphids, red spider mites and mealy bugs sometimes attack bougainvilleas.

Flowering bougainvillea with its vivid pink bracts – these enclose the white 'true' flowers

73

HEDERA CANARIENSIS*

Hedera canariensis 'Variegata', the Canary Island ivy, is a highly variegated, large leaved ivy that is most hardy and grows very well in a cool greenhouse. The leaves are a beautiful blend of creamy-white and deep green, borne on red stems. The plant climbs well, requiring only a little support, for it tends to anchor itself on any suitable ledge or crevice that offers itself in the greenhouse. It can reach 6 metres (20 ft) in height in exceptional cases. Obviously you would cut it back before it came to this!

General Care: The Canary Island ivy should be grown in a well-lit position, although it will tolerate a little shade. As far as watering in summer is concerned, the plant may be allowed to dry out a little before being re-watered. During the winter the plant should, however, be kept on the dry side when it will tolerate temperatures down to 4°C (40°F). If the plant is kept too moist during the winter, it will become susceptible to root rot. Occasional trimming, even quite active pruning back, will encourage the plant to remain in a reasonably tidy shape. Grow it in 10-15 cm (4-6 inch) pots of John Innes No. 2 potting compost, or a soil-less compost. Feed monthly with a diluted liquid fertilizer in summer.

Propagation: Canary Island ivy can be propagated by stem cuttings in July. Take pieces of stem, each with about two or three leaves and about 3 cm (1¼ inches) of stem below the bottom leaf. Dip each piece

into hormone rooting powder and insert approximately five to a 9 cm (3½ inch) pot of potting compost. Cover with polythene or mist with water occasionally to reduce water loss. Grow on in the pot after rooting.

Pests and Diseases: The plant may suffer from red spider mites, aphids, mealy bugs, and root mealy bugs.

HOYA*

The hoya, sometimes called the porcelain plant, is a succulent that has fleshy leaves borne on woody stems. The plant's rather untidy growth habit is its only real failing; the

Flowering hoya (the porcelain plant)

beautiful white flowers of the hoya are often borne in clusters about 10 cm (4 inches) across, and look like a work of art created from porcelain – hence the plant's common name. It flowers from May to September.

General Care: Hoya needs substantial support, requiring a good trellis or wire and cane frame. It also dislikes too much direct light, preferring light shade. It is important to get the watering right, for this may be crucial to success. During the spring and summer, the plant should be kept relatively moist, although it must be allowed to dry out a little in between waterings. However, over winter the plant should be kept on the dry side when it will tolerate temperatures down to around 10°C (50°F).

Bud or flower drop may occur if there are severe temperature fluctuations or major changes in soil moisture content. Grow in 25-30 cm (10-12 inch) pots of John Innes No. 2 potting compost or a soil-less compost. Feed every three weeks with dilute liquid fertilizer in summer.

Propagation: Hoyas can be propagated by stem cuttings in June, each with one, two or three pairs of leaves. Dip the bottom of each stem cutting into hormone rooting powder and insert about three to a 9 cm (3½ inch) pot of seed compost. Grow on in the pot.

Pests and Diseases: Hoya is subject to attack by mealy bugs and root mealy bugs.

JASMINE*

Jasminum polyanthum, or indoor jasmine, makes a most attractive and easy to grow plant for the cool greenhouse. The dark green, finely cut foliage climbs well, provided the plant has reasonable support. In early spring the plant covers itself with the most attractive and exquisitely scented white flowers that last for a number of weeks. It grows to a height of 1.5-3 metres (5-10 ft).

General Care: Jasmine adapts well to either a well-lit, or slightly shaded, situation. It requires moderate support and can even be grown on a hoop if so desired. During spring and summer, take great care to ensure that the plant remains moist and is not allowed to dry out. Once it has finished flowering, the plant may be occasionally trimmed and trained. Surprisingly, it will grow at a tremendous rate once it has flowered and needs to be kept in check to prevent it taking over!

In winter the plant should be kept cool, at around 5-7°C (41-45°F) and a little drier than during the summer. It can be grown in the greenhouse border or in 25-30 cm (10-12 inch) pots of John Innes No. 2 potting compost.

Propagation: Jasmine can easily be propagated in March or September from top or stem cuttings dipped into hormone rooting powder and inserted three to a 9 cm (3½ inch) pot of seed compost. If small plants are preferred, cuttings taken in March can be potted up into 13 cm (5 inch) pots and discarded after flowering.

Pests and Diseases: Aphids tend to be the major pest of jasmine, particularly in the spring when the plant is flowering, or when it is generating new growth.

Jasmine (Jasminum polyanthum)

PASSIFLORA*

The passiflora, far better known as the passion flower, is a very bold plant with deep green leaves and curling tendrils that help it climb up to 9 metres (30 ft) in exceptional cases. The growth is vigorous and the abundance of greenery provides a mass of cover. The plant is at its best, however, when it produces its most unusual and beautifully spectacular flowers. Occasionally the plant will fruit under glass, particularly if it flowers freely.

General Care: Passion flowers grow in a well-lit situation, although they prefer a little light shade. Watering through the spring and summer is important and the plants must not be allowed to dry out, particularly when they are in flower, otherwise the buds and flowers are likely to drop prematurely.

During the winter, passion flowers should be kept on the dry side and will happily tolerate temperatures down to about 2°C (35°F). The plants will need to be kept in check and should be trimmed or pruned from time to time to stop them taking over the greenhouse!

Grow them in the greenhouse border or in 25-30 cm (10-12 inch) pots of John Innes No. 3 potting compost.

Propagation: Passion flowers are easily raised from seed germinated in spring at about 20°C (68°F). The seedlings should be pricked out and potted up singly in 9 cm (3½ inch) pots of potting compost when large enough to handle.

Alternatively they can be propagated from stem cuttings in July. Dip the stems into hormone rooting powder, then insert into pots of seed compost, three to a 9 cm (3½ inch) pot. Keep at about 20°C (68°F), and in a humid atmosphere until rooted.

Pests and Diseases: Passion flowers are sometimes attacked by aphids, mealy bugs and red spider mites.

STEPHANOTIS**

In many ways, stephanotis are similar to hoyas. Their leaves, flowers and even habit of growth are similar. The plants have deep green fleshy succulent leaves on woody stems, while the flowers are larger than those of the hoya but are fleshy and wax-like in appearance. The scent is absolutely amazing and makes these plants well worth growing in your greenhouse. They can reach 3 metres (10 ft) if trained up strings or canes.

General Care: Although stephanotis like a certain amount of sunlight, too much sun may scorch the leaves, so light shading may be necessary. Provide a minimum temperature of 18°C (64°F) in the summer. During spring and summer, keep the plants moist; do not let them dry out as this could cause the flowers and/or buds to drop.

Passiflora (passion flower)

In winter, the plants should be kept on the dry side, at a temperature not lower than 10°C (50°F). Apart from being trained up stakes or along wires, stephanotis can also be grown well on a hoop of wire. Grow them in 13 cm (5 inch) pots of John Innes No. 2 potting compost, or a soil-less compost. They can be grown in large tubs or in the greenhouse border if large plants are required. Feed every two weeks in summer with dilute liquid fertilizer.

Propagation: Stephanotis can be propagated from cuttings. Take these in May, dip into hormone rooting powder, then insert into seed compost and maintain at a temperature of about 18°C (65°F) until rooted. Pot up into 9 cm (3½ inch) pots of potting compost. Soft, young plant growth is not suitable for propagation purposes and it is therefore better to use the more mature stems as cuttings.

Pests and Diseases: Mealy bugs are probably the most common pest.

THUNBERGIA*

The thunbergia grown as a climbing or trailing greenhouse plant is also known as Black-eyed Susan. It produces a mass of colourful golden orange flowers with a brownish-black 'eye' at the centre of the flower. Unfortunately the foliage is rather bland and it is only the flowers that are appealing. Because the plant is an annual it dies after flowering. It will grow to 3 metres (10 ft) in exceptional cases.

General Care: Black-eyed Susan is easy to grow and can even be grown outside when all risk of frost has passed. The plant should be supplied with canes or wires to support its rather feeble, leggy growth and should be placed in a well-lit position. Water freely and do not allow the plant to dry out at any time. Grow it in 15-20 cm (6-8 inch) pots of John Innes No. 2 potting compost.

Propagation: Thunbergia is propagated from seed sown in March. To avoid root disturbance, it is better to sow directly

Thunbergia (Black-eyed Susan)

into a small pot of seed compost, sowing between three and five seeds in a 9 cm (3½ inch) pot. Thin to one per pot later. Germinate at about 20°C (68°F) and grow on in the pot. Pot up as necessary using potting compost.

Pests and Diseases: Thunbergia may be attacked by aphids and white fly.

INDEX

Abutilon 72
African violet 24,25,59,*59*,61
Agave 30
Agave americana 30,*31*
All-purpose compost 18
Aloe 30-1
Aloe variegata 30
Alpine strawberry 70
Aluminium greenhouses 6
Aluminium plant 40-1,*41*
Aluminium shelving 8
Amaryllis 44,*45*
Ants 29
Aphids 29
Apricot 62,*63*
Araucaria 31
Araucaria excelsa 31
Asparagus fern 32,*32*
Asparagus plumosus 32
Asparagus sprengeri 32,*32*
Aspidistra 32,*33*
Asplenium 33
Asplenium nidus avis 33
Astilbe 44-5
Aubergine 63
Automatic watering systems 14
Azalea 45
Azalea indica 45

Begonia 22,44,45-6,*46*
Begonia rex 24,25,33-4
Bellflower 48
Benches 8
Bird's nest fern 33
Black-eyed Susan 77,*77*
Blackfly 29
Blinds 11,*11*
Botrytis 29
Bougainvillea 72-3,*73*
Bryophyllums 25
'Bubble plastic' 10
Bulbs 21,44,46-7
Busy Lizzie 56,*56*

Cabbage lettuce 66
Cacti 27,51-2,56-7,58-9,60
Calceolaria 20,47,*47*
Campanula 48
Campanula isophylla 48
Canary Island ivy 74
Cantaloupe melon 66
Cape primrose 61,*61*
Capillary watering system 14,18

Carnation 44,48-9,*48*
Caterpillars 29
Celosia 49,*49*
Chicory 20,21
Chinese rose 54
Chlorophytum 25,34
Chlorophytum comosum 34,*34*
Choosing a greenhouse 4,6
Chrysanthemum 44,50,*50*
Cineraria 20,50-1
Circular greenhouse 4
Clay pots 16,22
Climbing plants 72-7
Cockscomb 49,*49*
Coleus 34-5,*35*
Composts 18-19,25
Concrete flooring 10
Corrugated asbestos bench-tops 8
Cos lettuce 66
Courgette 62,63-4
Creeping fig 37-8
Crisphead lettuce 66
Crocus 21,46,47
Cucumber 8,20,62,64,*64*
Cut-and-come-again lettuce 66
Cuttings 22,24-5
Cyclamen 20,44,51,*51*
Cyperus 35
Cyperus alternifolius 35

Daffodil 46,47
Damping off 29
Desert privet 40
Dianthus 48-9
Dibber 16
Diseases and pests 28-9
Division, propagation by 22,25
Double glazing 10
Drainage 27
'Drip' principle watering devices 14
Duck-boards 10

Earwigs 29
Easter cactus 58
Echeveria 36
Echinopsis 51-2
Electrical heaters 12,*12*,13
Electricity supply to greenhouse 14
Epiphyllum 52
Euonymus 36-7
Euonymus radicans 36

Fan heaters 12,*12*,14
Fatshedera 37
Fatshedera lizei 36,37

Feeding decorative plants 27-8
Ferns 25,30
Fertilizer spikes 28
Fertilizers 28
Ficus elastica 38,*38*
Ficus pumila 37-8,*37*
Flame nettle 34-5
Flooring 10
Flowering maple 72
Flowering plants 44-61
Foliage plants 30-43
Free-standing greenhouse 4,6
Fruit and vegetables 62-71
Fuchsia 44,*52*,53
Fumigation 28
Fungus gnat 29

Geranium 44,53-4,*53*
Glazing 6-7
Granular fertilizers 28
Grape 62,65-6,*65*
Greenfly 29
Greenhouse:
    benches and shelving for a 8
    choosing a 4,6
    flooring for a 10
    glazing a 6-7
    heating the 4,12-13
    insulation of the 10
    shading the 11
    siting the 4
    size and shape of 6
    types of 4,6
    ventilation for the 7,10-11
    wood or metal-framed 6
Grey mould 29
Growing bags 19,62
Gutters 7
Gynura 38-9

Heating the greenhouse 4,12-13
Hedera canariensis 74
Hibiscus 54
Hibiscus rosa-sinensis 54
Hippeastrum 44,*45*
Home-made composts 19
Hormone rooting powder 24
Hoya 72,74-5,*74*
Hyacinth 46,47
Hydrangea 44,54-5,*54-5*

Impatiens 44,56,*56*
Indian azalea 45
Insulation 10
Ivy 24,74
Ivy-leaved pelargonium 53

Jasmine 75,*75*

Jasminum polyanthum 75,*75*
John Innes composts 18,19,22,26

Leaf-but cuttings 24
Leaf cuttings 24-5,*24*
Leaf miners 29
Leaf spot 29
Lean-to greenhouse 4,*4*,6
Lettuce 62,66,*66*
Liquid fertilizer 28
'Liquid shading' 11
Loam-based composts 18-19
Louvre vents 7

Mammillaria 56-7
Mealy bugs 29
Melon 20,62,66-7,*67*
Metal-framed greenhouse 6
Mildew 29
Mini-cyclamen 51
Mini-plants 25
Mist propagators 14
Monstera 39
Monstera deliciosa 39,*39*
Mother-in-law's-tongue
    25,42-3,*43*
Mustard and cress 67

Narcissi 21,46,47
Nitrogen 28
Norfolk Island pine 31

Ogen melon 66,*67*
Orchid cactus 52
Overwatering 27

Palms 30
Paraffin heaters 12,*12*,13
Partridge-breasted aloe 30
Passiflora (Passion flower)
    72,76,*76*
Peach 62,68,*68*
Peat-based composts 18
Peat 'pellets' 18
Peat pots and blocks
    16,*16*,18,26,*26*
Pelargonium 53-4,*53*
Peperomia magnoliaefolia 40,*40*
Peppers 62,68-9,*69*
Pests and diseases 28-9
Philodendron scandens 40
Pilea cadierei 40-1,*41*
Pineapple 69
Pittosporum 41
Planning what to grow 20-1
Plant labels 16
Plantlets 22,25,*25*
Plastic pots 16

Plastic seed trays 18
Platycerium 42
Platycerium bifurcatum 42,*42*
Polyanthus 44,57,*57*
Polypropylene pots 16
Polythene glazing 6-7
Polythene sheeting double
    glazing 10,*10*
Porcelain plant 74-5,*74*
Potash 28
Pots 16-17,62
Potting compost 18,19
Potting on 26-7,*27*
Potting up 26
Presser board 16
Pricking out 25-6,*25*
Primula 20
Propagation 22-6,*24-5*
Propagators 13,*13*,14
Propane gas heaters 12,*12*,13
Pruning grapes 65

Queen of the night 60

Rebutia 58,*58*
Red spider mites 29
Regal pelargonium 53
Rhipsalidopsis 58-9
Rhipsalidopsis gaertneri 58-9
Rhubarb 21,62,70,*70*
Root aphids 29
Root mealy bugs 29
Rooting cuttings 25
Rubber plant 38
Runner bean 4

Saintpaulia 59,*59*,61
Sand bench 14
Sansevieria 42-3
Sansevieria trifasciata 'Laurentii'
    42,*43*
Scale insects 29
Sciarid 29
Seed or sowing compost
    18,19,22,*22*,25
Seed trays 18,22,26
Seeds, to sow 22,24
Selenicereus 60
Selenicereus grandiflorus 60
Semi-automatic watering
    systems 14,27
Senecio cruentus 50-1
Shading the greenhouse 11
Shape of greenhouse 4,*4*,6
Shelving 8
Silver-leaved cyclamen 51
· Siting the greenhouse 4
Size of greenhouse 6

Slatted blinds 11
Slow-release fertilizers 19
Smoke cone 28,*28*
Soil-less composts 18,19,26,27
Soil-warming cables 13,14
Solanum 44,60
Solanum capsicastrum 60,*60*
Sowing seeds 22,*22*,24
Spider plant 25,*25*,34,*34*
Spirea 44-5
Split-canes 16
Sprayer 16
St Bernard lily 34
Stag's horn fern 42,*42*
Steel-framed greenhouse 6
Stem cuttings 24,*24*
Stephanotis 72,76-7
Strawberry 62,70
Streptocarpus 25,61,*61*
Succulents 27
Sweet corn 4
Sweetheart plant 40
Swiss cheese plant 39,*39*

Thrips 29
Thunbergia 77,*77*
Tomato 8,20,21,26,62,70-1,*71*
Tomato fertilizer 28
Tradescantia 43
Tree-living fern 42
Tubular heaters 12
Tulip 46,47

Vegetables and fruit 62-71
Velvet nettle 38-9
Ventilation, ventilators
    7,*7*,10-11,*11*

Water supply to greenhouse 14
Water vapour 12,13
Watering 27
Watering-can 15,16
Watering devices 14
Whitefly 28,29
Winter cherry 60,*60*
Wooden-framed greenhouse 6
Wooden shelving 8

Zonal pelargonium 53

ACKNOWLEDGEMENTS

Special Photography by Neil Holmes

Illustrations by artists from The Garden Studio : Christine
Davison 16, 20, 22, 24-28; Heather Dew 12-13, 15, 18-19;
Josephine Martin 4, 7, 8, 10-11.

The publishers also wish to thank the following
photographers and organizations for their kind permission
to reproduce the photographs in this book :
A-Z Botanical Collection 57, 58; Michael Boys/Octopus
Books Ltd. 1, 5, 9, 17, 66, 67; Octopus Books Ltd. 51, 60;
Harry Smith Horticultural Photographic Collection 45, 63;
George Wright/Octopus Books Ltd. 23, 64.